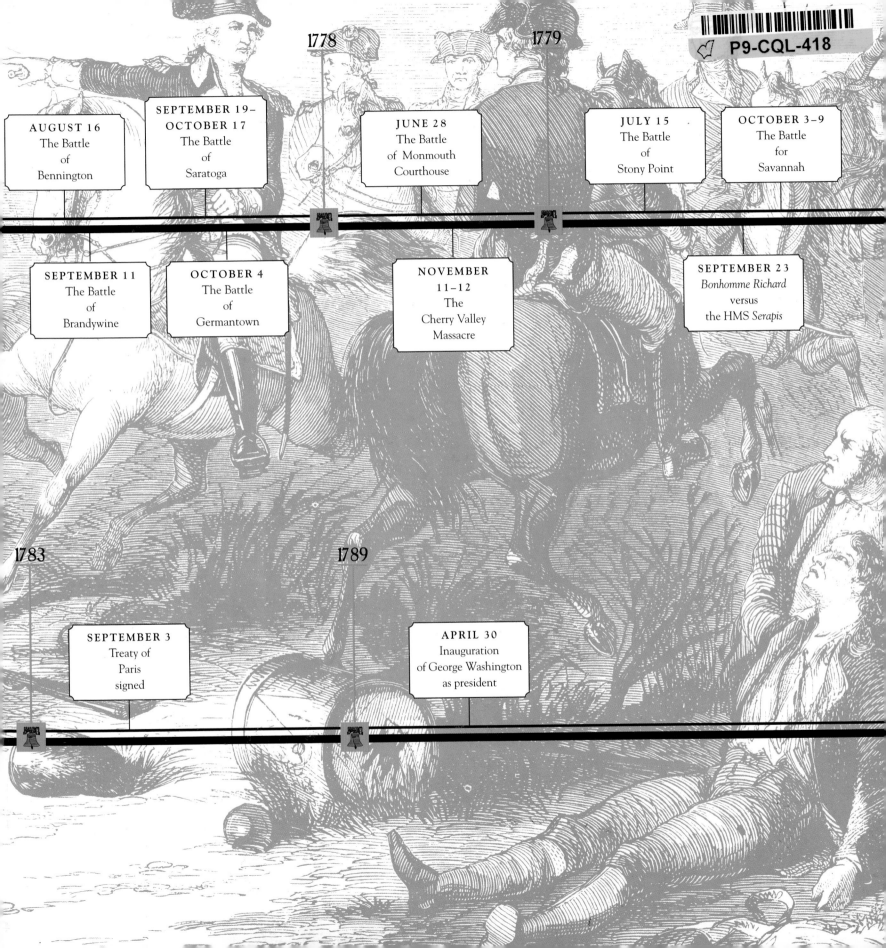

1778

1779

AUGUST 16
The Battle
of
Bennington

**SEPTEMBER 19–
OCTOBER 17**
The Battle
of
Saratoga

JUNE 28
The Battle
of Monmouth
Courthouse

JULY 15
The Battle
of
Stony Point

OCTOBER 3–9
The Battle
for
Savannah

SEPTEMBER 11
The Battle
of
Brandywine

OCTOBER 4
The Battle
of
Germantown

**NOVEMBER
11–12**
The
Cherry Valley
Massacre

SEPTEMBER 23
Bonhomme Richard
versus
the HMS *Serapis*

1783

1789

SEPTEMBER 3
Treaty of
Paris
signed

APRIL 30
Inauguration
of George Washington
as president

FIGHT FOR FREEDOM

✶ THE AMERICAN ✶
REVOLUTIONARY WAR

BENSON BOBRICK

A Byron Preiss Visual Publications, Inc. Book

ATHENEUM BOOKS FOR YOUNG READERS

NEW YORK LONDON TORONTO SYDNEY

To my late, great friend, L. Prospect Katz, tough as nails

Atheneum Books for Young Readers
An imprint of Simon & Schuster Children's Publishing Division
1230 Avenue of the Americas
New York, New York 10020

Front jacket photo caption: The Death of General Mercer at the Battle of Princeton, January 3, 1777 *by John Trumbull, copyright © Francis G. Mayer/CORBIS*
Title page photo caption: Bonhomme Richard *vs* HMS Serapis

The text of this book is set in Goudy.

Manufactured in the United States of America

10 9 8 7 6 5 4 3 2

Library of Congress Cataloging–in–Publication Data
Bobrick, Benson, 1947–
Fight for freedom : the American Revolutionary War /
Benson Bobrick.— 1st ed.
p. cm.
ISBN 0-689-86422-1
1. United States—History—Revolution, 1775–1783—Juvenile literature.
[1. United States—History—Revolution, 1775–1783.] I. Title.
E208.B6835 2004
973.3—dc22   2003025548

PHOTO CREDITS:
Bureau of Engraving and Printing: p. 24
Don Troiani, www.historicalartprints.com: pp. 13, 17, 41
Early American Digital Library: pp. 16, 34
Granger Collection, New York: p. 23
Independence National Historical Park: pp. 75, 76
Library of Congress: pp. 6, 8–11, 20 (*both*), 21, 22, 25–28, 30, 33, 35, 37–39, 47, 50, 51, 53, 55–57, 59, 60, 63, 67, 70 (*right*), 71, 73, 78, 79, 86, 87, 90
Louis S. Glanzman/National Geographic Image Collection: p. 61
Mark Stein: pp. 7, 31, 43, 83
Metropolitan Museum of Art, Gift of Col. and Mrs. Edgar William Garbisch, 1963. (63.201.2): p. 29
Mount Vernon Ladies' Association: p. 36
Murals Committee of Clarendon County Chamber of Commerce by Will Anderson: p. 49
National Archives: pp. 5, 15, 40, 45, 46, 48, 52, 62, 66, 68, 70 (*left*), 72, 74, 77, 88
National Park Service, Kings Mountain National Military Park: pp. 80 (*left*), 81
National Park Service, Morristown National Historical Park: pp. 32, 44, 58, 84
National Park Service, Museum Management Program and Guilford Courthouse National Military Park: pp. 42, 80 (*right*), 85
New York Historical Society: p. 91
New York State Office of Parks Recreation and Historic Preservation, Stony Point Battlefield State Historic Site: p. 65
Picture History: p. 89
State of South Carolina: p. 82
Thomas E. Kindig: p. 54

Contents

The American Revolution was the historic struggle by which the thirteen British colonies of North America gained independence from Great Britain and went on to create the United States. This great "fight for freedom" was inspired by certain ideals, and their triumph gave rise to our democratic form of government. The principles of that government, and the ideals on which it is based, are set forth in two immortal documents: the Declaration of Independence and the Constitution of the United States. These documents continue to stand today as the twin lights of liberty.

As the colonies began their rebellion, they felt it necessary to explain to the world why they had embarked on such a course. And so on July 4, 1776 they formally adopted a Declaration of Independence which set forth a theory of government which Americans have embraced ever since. The Declaration begins:

"We hold these truths to be self-evident, that all men are created equal, that they are endowed by their Creator with certain inalienable Rights, that among these are Life, Liberty, and the pursuit of Happiness. That to secure these rights, Governments are instituted among Men, deriving their just powers from the consent of the governed . . ."

These were lofty ideals—some people thought them unrealistic—and the colonists had to endure a brave and difficult war before they had a chance to show that these goals could work. The following pages describe the circumstances of that war—which is usually called the American Revolution and sometimes the War of Independence. It lasted longer than any other war in American history—eight years from the opening shots at Lexington and Concord in April of 1775 to the signing of the peace treaty in Paris in 1783. From scattered local resistance against an occupying force, the Revolution soon escalated into a full-fledged armed conflict that engulfed the entire Atlantic seaboard and involved some of the most powerful nations of Europe on either side.

There were many ups and downs to the war and many setbacks for the patriot army. The cause of freedom had many desperate days. It still seems almost a miracle that it triumphed in the end. One of the reasons it did is that several great leaders emerged to guide the fight. Today they are generally known as the Founding Fathers—George Washington, Thomas Jefferson, John Adams, and Alexander Hamilton, among others. A number of women also played important roles—for example, Abigail Adams, the wife of John Adams, who deserves to be called a Founding Mother because of her deep involvement in the issues of her day.

In *Fight for Freedom* you will also encounter such rebels as Paul Revere, an accomplished silversmith who became a household legend because of one night's historic ride; Ranger Daniel Morgan, a crack shot and guerilla warfare expert; outstanding statesmen such as Benjamin Franklin and Richard Henry Lee; and traitor Benedict Arnold, the biggest scoundrel of the war.

But among all participants, one man stands out above the rest. That man is George Washington, who has captured the imagination of Americans as our greatest hero and the one essential figure in our nation's birth. As a man of war, he proved steadfast and courageous. As a man of peace, he showed himself as wise a statesman as the world has ever seen.

While I was growing up, I loved to read about the early years of our country—not only about the Revolution, but about life in the colonies before the Revolution began. Strangely enough it wasn't until I was somewhat older that I discovered a number of my own ancestors were involved in the fighting. Most were Patriots and fought under George Washington in the Continental army. But several were Loyalists who sided with the king.

Quite a few families at the time were split in just this way. As the conflict wore on, brother was often set against brother, father against son. There was a great deal of suffering on both sides. Several of my relatives perished in the Revolution, and there is a strange story about one of them that I will never forget. He was a Patriot lad who lived with his mother

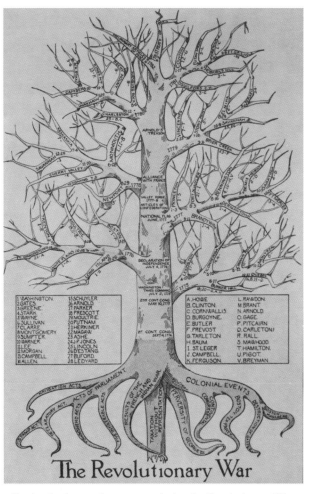

The Revolutionary War

Battles, leaders, and congresses during the Revolutionary War.

in New Jersey. He joined the Continental army, and it is said that after he went off to fight, his mother did not hear from him for a long time. Then one day as she was gazing out a window, she thought she saw him pass by. She was sure of it and called after him. But he rode on in silence and soon disappeared. Later she learned that at exactly the moment she had seen him, he had been killed in a battle far away.

The greatest story ever told may be that recounted in the Bible. But the second greatest, as far as the history of the world is concerned, is probably that of the American Revolution, when freedom and equality was established as the birthright of every human being on Earth.

Bruce Bahrick

Above: Engraving of King George III by R. H. Cromek.

Before the United States of America was formed, the British territories of New Hampshire, Massachusetts, Rhode Island, Connecticut, New York, New Jersey, Pennsylvania, Maryland, Delaware, Virginia, North Carolina, South Carolina, and Georgia were known as the "thirteen colonies." They were ruled by Great Britain, which was called the "mother country." In fact many European countries, including Britain's traditional rivals, France and Spain, had colonized America in the hopes of exploiting its natural wealth.

From the beginning, the colonies were regarded as a land of opportunity. In 1767 a rich plantation owner named George Washington noted the rich possibilities "in the back country for adventurers, where . . . an enterprising man with very little money may lay the foundation of a noble estate."

Though peppered with farms and cities, the land in all of the colonies was, for the most part, frontier wilderness. All the major cities, including Philadelphia, New York, Boston, Charleston, and Savannah, were located on the Atlantic coast. While the colonies were close to one another geographically, they were much closer economically to England, which was an ocean away. In fact by the 1760s, the American colonies accounted for about 12 percent of British imports and 25 percent of British exports.

For many years the colonists were happy under Britain's rule. In 1698 colonist Gabriel Thomas compared life in the Pennsylvania colony to that in England: "Corn and Flesh, and what else serves Man for Drink, Food and Rayment, is much cheaper here than in England, or elsewhere; but the chief reason why Wages of Servants of all sorts is much higher here than there, arises from the great Fertility and Produce of the Place; besides, if these large Stipends were refused them, they would quickly set up for themselves, for they can have Provision very cheap, and Land for a very small matter."

But this general feeling of contentment came to an end within a decade of the conclusion of the French and Indian War (fought from 1754–1763), the last great battle between Great Britain and France in North America. This war would have severe repercussions to the relationship between the thirteen colonies and Great Britain, all of which would lead to the colonists taking control of their own lives.

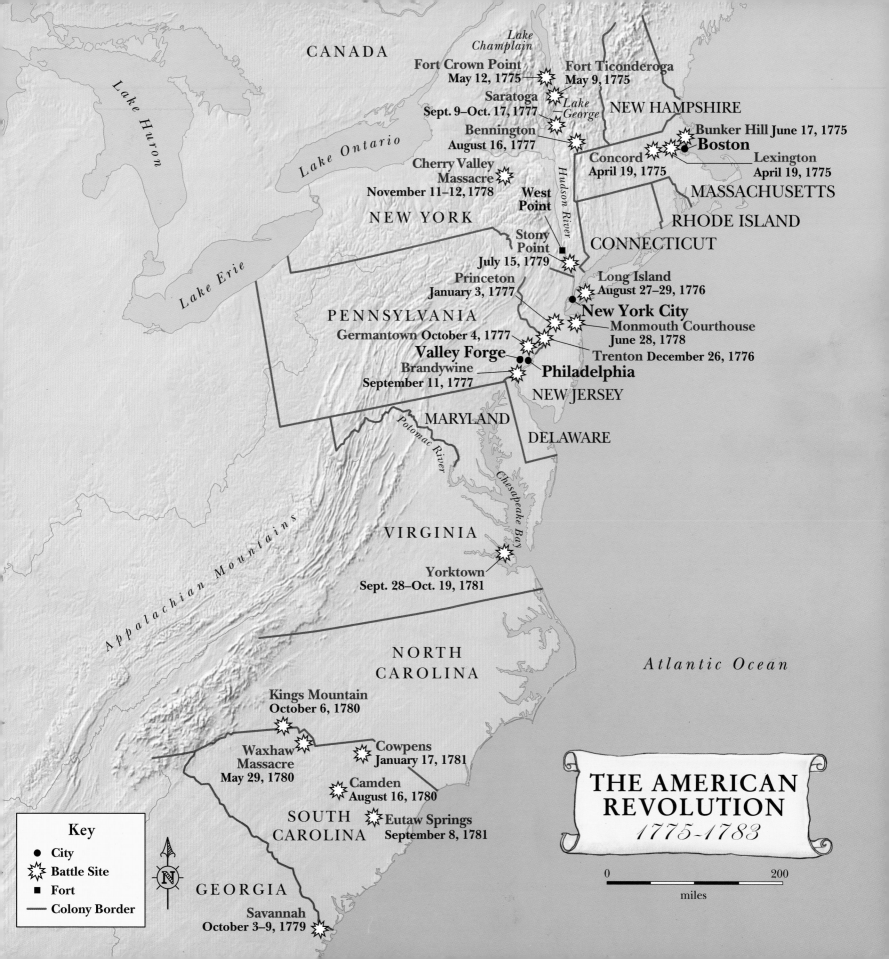

CANADA

Lake Champlain

Fort Crown Point
May 12, 1775

Fort Ticonderoga
May 9, 1775

Saratoga
Sept. 9–Oct. 17, 1777

Lake George

NEW HAMPSHIRE

Bennington
August 16, 1777

Bunker Hill June 17, 1775

Boston

Concord
April 19, 1775

Lexington
April 19, 1775

Cherry Valley
Massacre
November 11–12, 1778

MASSACHUSETTS

Hudson River

West
Point

RHODE ISLAND

NEW YORK

Stony
Point
July 15, 1779

CONNECTICUT

Long Island
August 27–29, 1776

Princeton
January 3, 1777

New York City

Monmouth Courthouse
June 28, 1778

PENNSYLVANIA

Germantown October 4, 1777

Valley Forge

Trenton December 26, 1776

Brandywine
September 11, 1777

Philadelphia

NEW JERSEY

MARYLAND

DELAWARE

Potomac River

Chesapeake Bay

VIRGINIA

Yorktown
Sept. 28–Oct. 19, 1781

Atlantic Ocean

Appalachian Mountains

NORTH
CAROLINA

Kings Mountain
October 6, 1780

Waxhaw
Massacre
May 29, 1780

Cowpens
January 17, 1781

Camden
August 16, 1780

SOUTH
CAROLINA

Eutaw Springs
September 8, 1781

Key

● City
✸ Battle Site
■ Fort
— Colony Border

N

GEORGIA

Savannah
October 3–9, 1779

**THE AMERICAN
REVOLUTION**
1775-1783

0   200
miles

Lake Huron

Lake Ontario

Lake Erie

Above: A 1766 cartoon that depicts the funeral procession of the Stamp Act.

The seeds of the American Revolution were planted during the French and Indian War. When that war ended in 1763, the victorious British took control of all the French territory in North America. That territory included Canada and stretched from the Atlantic coast to the Mississippi River. But the war had been very expensive, and with the victory, the British had also acquired a huge mountain of debt.

The British Parliament, with King George III's backing, expected the colonists to help pay for the war and for the additional soldiers needed to keep order along the new frontiers. Without consulting the colonists, Parliament began to impose taxes upon them and found other ways to intrude on their lives. The Quartering Act of 1765 forced the colonists to provide food, shelter, and supplies to the troops. This act was followed by the Stamp Act of 1765, which was a tax on a wide variety of official documents as well as newspapers, calendars, and playing cards. Once the tax was paid, the item received an official ink stamp, much like the customs stamp on a passport today. The Townsend Acts of 1767 were designed to raise revenue to pay the salaries of British government officials in America.

The Americans were outraged. Patrick Henry, a member of Virginia's colonial government, the House of Burgesses, eloquently declared: "Taxation without representation is tyranny." This statement became the rallying cry of a widening protest that took the British Parliament by surprise.

Over the span of a decade, the divide between the colonies and Great Britain grew. The core issue continued to be who had the right to tax the colonists and make the laws they were supposed to obey. Parliament and King George III claimed they did, but the American colonists asserted that unless they were represented in Parliament, the British government had no such right. Agitation against British rule increased and began to express itself in open rebellion. One of the first such acts led to the Boston Massacre.

The Boston Massacre started with a confrontation between some Bostonians and a British sentry that quickly drew a crowd. When the sentry called for help, a group of eight armed British soldiers led by Captain Thomas Preston came to his aid. By then a mob had gathered, taunting the

Opposite: Engraving of *The Bloody Massacre Perpetrated in King Street, Boston on March 5, 1770* by Paul Revere.

Above: The Boston Tea Party.

soldiers and throwing rocks and sticks at them. Accounts of what exactly happened next differ. What is known for certain is that at one point the soldiers panicked and fired into the mob. Five colonists were killed and several others were wounded. News of the incident spread quickly. Samuel Adams, who belonged to a Patriot group known as the Sons of Liberty, asked Paul Revere, a silversmith and fellow Patriot, to engrave a picture of the scene. This engraving was printed and sent throughout the colonies, further igniting anti-British sentiment.

A few years later, in 1773, there was a protest of a different kind. The Boston Tea Party, as it came to be known, was a protest over a new tax on tea. The tax itself was small, but King George III and Parliament wanted to prove that they could impose any tax on the colonists they wished. To the Americans, it was just another example of taxation without representation. So, in Boston a group of Patriots decided to dress themselves up as Native Americans, board the British tea ships in the harbor, and dump all their cargo of tea into the water. When they were finished, 342 chests of British-owned tea had been thrown overboard. This act was a very daring but peaceful protest. Nobody was hurt, and nothing else on the ships was damaged or destroyed.

Still, King George III was furious. He demanded that Parliament pass a series of laws designed to punish the people of Boston and at the same time intimidate the rest of the colonies. These laws were called the Restraining Acts, or the Coercive Acts. The colonists called them the Intolerable Acts. In effect, the acts placed the colony of Massachusetts under British army rule. All officials received their direct appointments from London, and the citizens of Massachusetts no longer had much say in their affairs. The colonists could not even hold a town meeting without first getting special permission to do so.

But instead of being intimidated, the other colonies rallied to the Patriot cause. They sent representatives to the city of Philadelphia, where, on September 5, 1774, a Continental Congress convened to formally protest the Intolerable Acts and to plan measures of collective resistance, including a framework of mutual assistance and response.

At the same time that the Americans were meeting, Parliament was trying to decide exactly what it should do next. During one of its many debates, Colonel Isaac Barre of the British army warned that if Parliament did not act wisely and justly, the colonies would soon have "their date of independence," and be totally free of English rule whether England liked it or not.

On April 19, 1775, in the Massachusetts towns of Lexington and Concord, his prediction began to come true.

Opposite: Portrait of Patrick Henry by George Bagby Matthews.

The Battle of Lexington and Concord

Quick Facts

🔔 Paul Revere was a silversmith by trade. Though he was smart, resourceful, and courageous, he owes part of his fame to Henry Wadsworth Longfellow's poem "The Midnight Ride of Paul Revere," which both exaggerated and immortalized what he did.

🔔 Governor Patrick Henry of Virginia was one of the greatest orators of his time. He was a delegate to the first Continental Congress, and in one of his speeches to the Congress, he had proudly stated, "I am not a Virginian, but an American!" People picked up on that, and though most Americans at the time considered themselves citizens of their own colony, they also began to think of themselves as Americans.

🔔 An elderly woman by the name of Mother Batherick lived near Concord at the time of the battle. She happened to be digging weeds in a pond when, hearing a noise, she looked up and found herself facing six breathless, unarmed British soldiers who were trying to flee. The terrified men surrendered to her. After she turned the soldiers over to the minutemen, colonists liked to joke, "If one old lady can capture six [British soldiers], how many soldiers will King George need to conquer America?"

In response to the Boston Tea Party, British Prime Minister Lord North ordered the port of Boston closed and placed under the rule of the British general Thomas Gage and his army stationed there. With British troops now garrisoned in Boston, emotions were running high throughout the colonies. Even the Tories, or Loyalists, those loyal to the British crown, were angry at the way Parliament was handling things. But while the Tories wanted to find a peaceful way to settle the differences, radical groups were preparing to fight.

These Rebels began to stockpile a large store of guns and ammunition in the nearby town of Concord. When General Gage heard about it, he ordered a detachment of men led by Major John Pitcairn to seize it, and if possible, to capture any Rebel leaders that they could find.

Through spies and other espionage methods, the British plans were discovered, and Patriot riders Paul Revere, William Dawes, and Dr. Samuel Prescott managed to slip out of Boston to spread the word. They successfully warned their associates to hide their weapons and munitions, and also to prepare themselves for a possible British attack. Revere was actually captured outside Lexington but then escaped from British troops. The Rebel minutemen, so-called because they could answer the call to arms at a minute's notice, were therefore ready when the British arrived. At Lexington, Maj. John Pitcairn and his men encountered a local group of them led by Captain John Parker. Parker had told his men, "Stand your ground. Don't fire unless fired upon. But if they want to have a war, let it begin here."

The situation was tense. The minutemen were determined not to let the British advance to Concord. The British were just as determined to do their duty. Maj. Pitcairn ordered, "Lay down your arms, you damned rebels, and disperse!" The Rebels slowly began backing away. Then, suddenly, a shot was fired. To this day, no one knows who fired that fateful shot, but it became famous as "the shot heard 'round the world."

The British troops immediately discharged a volley into the ranks of the militia, killing eight men. The minutemen retreated, and the British reached Concord. But the ammunition and guns once stocked there were gone, hidden in new locations in the region. News of the encounter electrified the colonies. The die was now cast. The Revolution had begun.

Opposite: The Battle of Lexington and Concord.

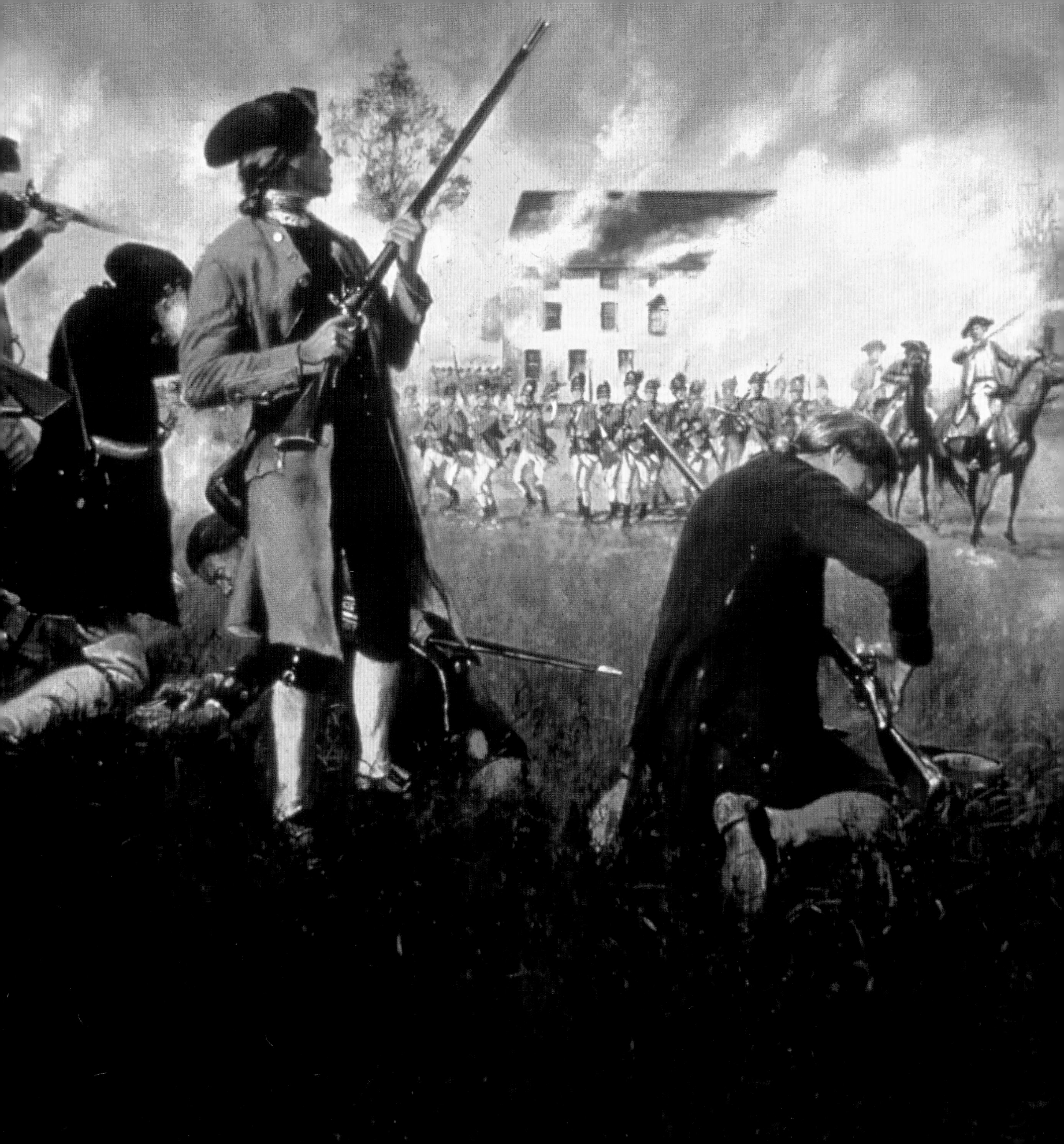

For the revolution against the British to succeed, the Rebels needed many things, especially guns, cannons, and ammunition for troops rallying to the cause. In May 1775, Benedict Arnold, one of the Patriot leaders from Connecticut, met with the rebel leaders of Massachusetts and told them that many such vital munitions were stockpiled at the British forts of Ticonderoga and Crown Point, which were on the border between New York and Vermont. Arnold was made a colonel in the Massachusetts militia, and led a force of four hundred men to seize the forts, which were known to be weakly defended. In particular he hoped to capture the "eighty pieces of heavy cannon, twenty brass guns . . . and ten to twelve large mortars" at Fort Ticonderoga.

As Arnold neared the fort, he met Patriot colonel Ethan Allen with his own Vermont militia known as the Green Mountain Boys. As it turned out, Allen had independently come up with the same idea as Arnold. Arnold and Allen did not get along, but they decided to set aside their differences and work together to ensure success.

On the evening of May 9, they launched a surprise attack, and almost before the small British garrison of only forty men realized it, Arnold, Allen, and their men had broken into the fort.

The astonished British commander was called out of bed. Holding his breeches in one hand, he asked by whose authority Allen was demanding the fort's surrender. The impetuous and energetic Allen said, "In the name of the great Jehovah and the Continental Congress!"

At first the British officer didn't know what to say. Then Arnold stepped up and said, "Give up your arms and you'll be treated like gentlemen." The British commander then agreed. In fact the arsenal at Fort Ticonderoga proved larger than Arnold's estimate; more than one hundred pieces of artillery and muskets were seized.

Arnold and Allen next moved to strike against Crown Point. On May 12, the thirteen British soldiers manning that fort surrendered without any resistance. Five days later, the militia followed up this raid with a third attack on a small fort at Saint Johns, capturing more cannon and small arms.

These three easy conquests gave a big boost to the Patriot cause—and hearts—to the Rebels in their fight.

Opposite: Colonel Ethan Allen demanding the surrender of Fort Ticonderoga.

Quick Facts

🔔 The Battle of Bunker Hill was actually fought on Breed's Hill which is located just south of Bunker Hill. The colonists, marching toward Bunker Hill at night, got lost and discovered in the morning that they were on Breed's Hill instead.

🔔 The Patriot soldiers were so short on bullets that some troops shot small pieces of iron and old nails from their muzzle loaders.

🔔 One of the reasons why the Patriots were able to inflict so many casualties on the British troops is that many were frontiersmen who had rifles which were more accurate at long ranges than the standard British musket.

🔔 At the Battle of Bunker Hill, General Israel Putnam and other Patriot officers issued the now famous command, "Don't shoot until you see the whites of their eyes."

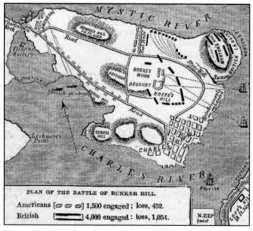

Above: The battle plan for the raid on Bunker Hill, where Americans lost 452 soldiers and the British lost 1,054.

ow substantially armed, the thirteen colonies were in open revolt. A second Continental Congress met in Philadelphia to decide what to do next. In the meantime, King George III ordered more troops to Boston, which was now surrounded by rebel militia ready and willing to take them on.

With the extra troops British general Thomas Gage planned to occupy the hills surrounding Boston, and then advance on the American camp at nearby Cambridge. The Americans learned of the plan and advanced their own volunteer soldiers to seize the same hills, focusing on the undefended peak of Bunker Hill. The sea was the British troops' supply lifeline. If colonial troops controlled the hills, their artillery could stop British supply ships from entering Boston Harbor.

On June 17, 1775, the British attacked. Thousands of people climbed onto rooftops or bell towers so that they could watch the battle. Everyone seemed to realize that what was being witnessed was not only a battle, it was the start of a war.

Gen. Gage peered through his spyglass at the Patriots and their entrenchments and asked his aide, "Who is that officer commanding?" The aide, a Loyalist, looked through the spyglass and recognized his own brother-in-law, Colonel William Prescott. Gage asked, "Well, will he fight?"

The aide replied, "Yes, sir, depend on it, to the last drop of blood in him, but I cannot answer for his men."

The men under Col. Prescott's command answered for themselves. Twice the British charged up the hill, and twice they were driven back by the Patriots' heavy and accurate fire. Despite heavy casualties, the British stubbornly attacked a third time. The Patriots had run out of ammunition and were forced to retreat.

Though the Patriot militia had been driven off Bunker Hill, they had gained the respect of the British commanders. General John Burgoyne observed, "The retreat was no flight; it was even covered with bravery and military skill." And Gen. Gage, in his report to the war ministry in London, wrote, "The Rebels are not the despicable rabble too many have supposed them to be." Soon after the Battle of Bunker Hill, the British troops in Boston found themselves under siege.

Right: The Patriots at the Battle of Bunker Hill.

Quick Facts

🔔 Three British regiments during the Revolutionary War were made up entirely of criminals whose crimes would be forgiven if they enlisted.

🔔 Mercenaries were very expensive because they were paid more than regular troops.

🔔 At the time of the American Revolution, Germany did not exist as a single country. It was a collection of small independent states, most of them ruled by monarchs. A total of six different German states sent mercenaries to America.

🔔 The standard firearm in the British army was a long-barreled musket called "Brown Bess." A musket is different from a rifle. Muskets are smooth-bore weapons, meaning the inside of the barrel is smooth. In a rifle the bore has grooves, which puts a spin on the bullet, improving its accuracy.

🔔 General George Washington, who was responsible for all Patriot troops regardless of affiliation, expressed his problem of command in one of his letters to Congress when he wrote, "If in all cases ours was one army, or thirteen armies allied for the common defense, there would be no difficulty . . . but we are occasionally both, and . . . sometimes neither, but a compound of both."

The soldiers on both sides of the war got their nicknames because of their uniforms. British soldiers sarcastically called the ill-equipped Rebel troops "Yankee Doodles," after an irreverent song of the time. The Americans called the British troops "Lobsterbacks" because their bright red coats were reminiscent of cooked lobsters.

The soldiers who served in the ranks of the American army had very little in common with troops in the British army. In America where so much of the land was frontier, average citizens had to be prepared to volunteer to help in the common defense against attack by Native Indian war parties. Britain, in contrast, kept a professional army that was trained in the art of European warfare. But the differences went even further.

There were three types of American soldiers: Continentals, militia, and state troops. The Continental army was a national army of enlistment that had formal rules and regulations, and an officer hierarchy. The militias and state troops were usually more loosely structured, and composed of groups of men from local communities who elected their own leaders and who also sometimes served as volunteers. Needless to say, it was often very hard to manage all three types of soldiers when they were thrown together.

Even so, they showed they could work together with a will. When the Continental army swiftly built fortifications around Boston, Gen. Gage was astonished. "My God! these fellows have done more work in one night than I could make my army do in three months."

The men who served in the ranks of the British army were recruited from the lowest levels of British society. Discipline was severe, and whipping was a common punishment. Officers, on the other hand, were from the upper classes. Many of them were noblemen who expected unquestioning obedience from their men. In addition the British government hired mercenaries—professional soldiers from other countries—to help fight in its wars. In the Revolutionary War the largest group of mercenaries were German troops called Hessians. Finally, there were the so-called Tories, or Loyalists—those colonials loyal to the king. Many of these Americans fought with the British in their campaigns.

Opposite: This engraving titled '76 by George W. Maynard, shows a Continental soldier in full uniform. The evergreen tree on the flag he is carrying suggests that the soldier is from New England.

 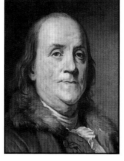

Above: John Jay (*left*) and Benjamin Franklin (*right*).

*N*ever before in history had so many individuals of such exceptional ability come together for one purpose as the leaders of the thirteen colonies. The list would come to include some of the most famous and influential men in American history. Several would become presidents; others would hold high office in the federal or state governments. The Continental Congress initially included George Washington, Thomas Jefferson, Patrick Henry, George Mason, members of the Lee family of Virginia; John and Samuel Adams, and John Hancock from Massachusetts; John Jay and Gouverneur Morris from New York; and Benjamin Franklin, John Dickinson, and Robert Morris from Pennsylvania, among others.

Most were men of wealth or professional distinction—that is, men of privilege, and so not the sort that one would expect to lead a rebellion. It is remarkable that despite their individual beliefs, they managed to unite for the cause of freedom. For example, John Jay was Conservative in his political beliefs, which meant he was cautious about instituting changes which would increase the power of the government; John Dickinson was a Moderate, a political stance which advocates a slow "wait-and-see" approach to change; Richard Henry Lee was a Radical, which means he embraced wide-sweeping rapid change; but they all fought for one goal.

Patrick Henry, during one of the first meetings of the Continental Congress, gave voice to the common purpose when he said: "All America is thrown into one mass. Where are your landmarks—your boundaries of colonies? They are all thrown down. The distinctions between Virginians, Pennsylvanians, New Yorkers, and New Englanders are no more. I am not a Virginian, but an American."

John Adams initially had doubts about some of the other members of the Continental Congress. But soon after its first meeting, he happily noted in his diary: "There is in the Congress a collection of the greatest men upon the continent in point of abilities, virtues, and fortunes. The magnanimity and public spirit which I see here make me blush."

Opposite, right to left: George Washington with Alexander Hamilton and Thomas Jefferson.

Quick Facts

🔔 No one knows exactly how many Loyalists there were. The best estimates range from 75,000 to 100,000 out of an estimated total population (in 1780) of 2,780,000. After the war at least 60,000 and perhaps as many as 80,000 Loyalists left the United States to live in England, Canada, or other countries. The largest group, about 35,000, settled in Nova Scotia, Canada, receiving a grant in land, clothing, and farm supplies from the British authorities.

🔔 Margaret Green Draper was the publisher of the Loyalist *Massachusetts Gazette* and *Boston Weekly News-Letter*. After the war her home and print shop were confiscated by the new American government. Draper left for Britain where, in recognition for her loyalty, the government gave her a pension.

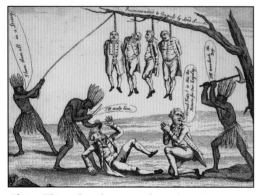

Above: This political cartoon shows America, represented by Native American Indians, killing six Loyalists.

ot everyone in the colonies wanted to break away from English rule. These people were called Loyalists, or Tories. They belonged to every rank and class. Some had close business or family ties to England. But many did not. Quite a few shared the outrage of the Patriots at such Parliamentary measures as the Stamp Acts, but they did not feel these measures justified a complete break from the British Empire.

Some of the Tories were related to Patriots. Indeed, many families were split apart due to political differences. William Franklin, the son of Benjamin Franklin, for example, was the last British governor of New Jersey and a staunch Loyalist. Thomas Jefferson's cousin John Randolph was a Tory and emigrated to England.

A number of Tories, like New York City's mayor, David Mathews, actively aided the British. After Patriots discovered Mathews' plot to raise a Loyalist force to help the British take over New York, Thomas Jones, a Tory judge, wrote: "A universal hunt after Loyalists took place. . . . The Loyalists were pursued like wolves and bears, from swamp to swamp, from one hill to another, from dale to dale, and from one copse of wood to another. In consequence . . . some were wounded, and a few murdered. The prisoners were . . . insulted and abused . . . [and] transported into different parts of New England."

As the war progressed, Tories found it more and more difficult to live in the colonies. In most areas, with the exception of places controlled by British armies, such as New York City, the Tories were harassed and persecuted, and their homes and businesses were seized.

When the war ended, many of the Loyalists went into exile in the Bahamas, the British West Indies, Canada, or England. George Washington and Alexander Hamilton tried to stop the exodus, because there were many well-educated and highly skilled people among them who would be needed to help build the new nation. Patrick Henry agreed, saying: "They have, to be sure, mistaken their own interests most woefully, and most woefully have they suffered the punishment due their offense. But the relations which we bear to them and to their native country are now changed. . . . The quarrel is over. Peace hath returned and found us a free people. Let us have the magnanimity to lay aside our antipathies and prejudices. . . ."

Most Tories, however, chose never to return.

Opposite: This image of forlorn and abandoned individuals shows the ultimate fate of many Loyalists.

Above: John Adams.

How did the First Continental Congress and the Second Continental Congress actually come about? When Parliament began enacting harsh laws against the colonists, the leaders of the thirteen colonies decided to form an advisory council called a congress, in order to discuss their common concerns and address Parliament with a single voice.

The First Continental Congress had met in Philadelphia in the fall of 1774 to formally protest the Coercive Acts, the measures Parliament had passed to punish the Massachusetts colony for the Boston Tea Party. Afterward the members adjourned and returned to their homes.

But Parliament rejected their protest, and after the Battle of Lexington and Concord, the Second Continental Congress met in Philadelphia in May 1775 to discuss what to do next. This was a very important meeting because the delegates took it upon themselves to decide whether or not to seek independence from Great Britain.

While they deliberated, Thomas Paine, an English-born, pro-independence radical living in Philadelphia, published a momentous pamphlet titled *Common Sense* on January 10, 1776. "We have it in our power to begin the world over again," he wrote, in a ringing appeal to many Americans who were sick of the old order and longed for a new form of government.

On June 7, 1776, Richard Henry Lee, a delegate from Virginia, rose and offered a vote of resolution that stated "[t]hat these United Colonies are, and of right ought to be, free and independent States, that they are absolved from all allegiance to the British Crown and that all political connection between them and the State of Great Britain is, and ought to be, totally dissolved."

Quickly John Adams from Massachusetts seconded the motion. Then delegates from seven other colonies voiced their support. The rest soon joined them. The thirteen colonies were now officially united in their desire for independence. All that was needed was a document that they could present to King George III and the British Parliament to confirm their stand—a declaration of independence.

Opposite: Four leaders of the Continental Congresses—John Adams, Gouverneur Morris, Alexander Hamilton, and Thomas Jefferson.

Quick Facts

🔔 Thomas Jefferson was born on the family plantation in Shadwell, Virginia. Because the land had been purchased for the price of a bowl of punch, it was called "the Punchbowl Tract."

🔔 Thomas Jefferson called politics a "hated profession." Even so, he became one of the most successful politicians of his time. He was a governor of Virginia, a secretary of state during George Washington's presidency, and later, president of the United States.

🔔 Thomas Jefferson and John Adams had a bitter falling out during Washington's first term as president, and the ill-will lasted for many years. Eventually mutual friends helped to bring about their reconciliation, which blossomed into a warm exchange of letters until they died on the same day, July 4, 1826.

Above: A painting of the signing of the Declaration of Independence that hangs in the U.S. Capitol.

Tall, thin, with light gray eyes, sharp features, and reddish hair, Thomas Jefferson was an extraordinary man among the group of extraordinary men who led the country during the American Revolution. His intellect and his curiosity were so vast that it seemed he could do anything and everything he set his mind to. He was an accomplished musician; an architect; was learned in botany, landscape design, cartography, meteorology, the caring and raising of livestock; and more. He was also an inventor. Among his inventions were the swivel chair, the retractable bed, and an adjustable tilt-top table.

At the beginning of the Revolution he was a Virginia plantation owner, a lawyer, a member of the House of Burgesses, and was famous as the writer of the eloquent pamphlet titled *A Summary View of the Rights of British America*, which condemned British oppression and stated the Patriot viewpoint. Because of this pamphlet, members of the Second Continental Congress felt Jefferson should be the one to write the Declaration of Independence. At first he tried to wriggle out of the assignment, and urged John Adams to pen the document. Years later Adams recounted the following exchange in which he tried to convince Jefferson to undertake the task:

"Reason, first, you are a Virginian and a Virginian ought to appear at the head of this business. Reason second, I am obnoxious, suspected, and unpopular. You are very much otherwise. Reason third, you can write ten times better than I can."

"Well," said Jefferson, "if you are decided, I will do as well as I can."

Three weeks later Jefferson presented his document to Congress. After some revisions the Declaration of Independence was officially adopted on July 4, 1776. Copies of it were then made and distributed throughout the colonies where it was read and greeted with enthusiastic acclaim.

John Adams, composing a letter to his wife, Abigail, wrote: "You will think me transported with Enthusiasm, but I am not—I am well aware of the Toil, and Blood, and Treasure it will cost Us to maintain this Declaration, and support and defend these States—Yet through all the gloom I can see the Rays of ravishing Light and Glory. I can see that the End is more than worth all the Means."

Opposite: Engraving of Thomas Jefferson holding the Declaration of Independence.

Quick Facts

🔔 George Washington did not take a salary while he was commander in chief of the Continental army. He asked only that his expenses be paid.

🔔 Washington was a bashful man. When John Adams nominated him for commander in chief, he blushed and rushed in embarrassment from the room.

🔔 A common misconception is that Washington had wooden false teeth. Over the years he had a number of dentures, but these were made from lead, hippopotamus ivory, and the teeth of animals, including cows—none of his teeth were made of wood.

Above: **Washington at his plantation in Mount Vernon, Virginia.**

The man who would come to be known as the "Father of His Country," George Washington, originally was a wealthy Virginia plantation owner. According to reports, he was a handsome man. At six feet two inches, he was tall, big-boned, and had a commanding presence. Washington was also well mannered—yet he had a terrible temper that he struggled all his life to control. While the story of young George Washington confessing to cutting down the cherry tree is a fabrication, Washington was scrupulously honest and smart. He avidly studied mathematics, and at the age of sixteen was part of a team that explored and mapped western Virginia. Commissioned a lieutenant colonel in 1754, he fought the initial skirmishes of the French and Indian War.

The Second Continental Congress voted unanimously to make George Washington the commander in chief of the Continental army on June 15, 1775. Washington, who had fought in the French and Indian War, had the most military experience of the group. Additionally, John Adams, who nominated Washington, said to the Congress in his nomination speech, "[his] skill as an officer, . . . great talents and universal character would command the respect of America and unite . . . the Colonies better than any other person alive."

Shortly after the vote was taken, Washington, a delegate from Virginia, put his feelings down in a private letter to his brother, John Augustine: "I have been called upon by the unanimous Voice of the Colonies to take the Command of the Continental Army—an honor I neither sought after, nor desired, as I am thoroughly convinced that it requires greater abilities, and more experience, than I am Master of . . . but the partiality of the Congress, joined to a political motive, really left me without a choice."

John Marshall, a close friend (and later a chief justice of the United States), said Washington had an "innate and unassuming modesty." In addition he said Washington was "endowed by nature with a sound judgment, and an accurate and discriminating mind."

The respect that the members of the Continental Congress had for Washington would grow as the Revolutionary War continued. When the war ended with a colonial victory, Washington would be unanimously elected the first president of the United States.

Opposite: **General George Washington and his staff reviewing the Continental army.**

Quick Facts

🔔 It was at New York Harbor that the colonists employed the world's first submarine, the *Turtle*. Invented by David Bushnell and piloted by Sergeant Ezra Lee, the *Turtle* ultimately failed in its mission to sink British ships.

🔔 Nathan Hale, a Patriot spy from New York City, was captured in September, shortly after the British had taken possession of the city. Before the British executed him, he uttered the immortal words, "I only regret that I have but one life to lose for my country."

🔔 The colonists were disheartened by the British success. "The morning on which the British troops landed," remembered one sixteen-year-old Dutch girl, ". . .[t]he sky was so clear and bright that you could scarcely think of it as a day which was to bring so much sorrow."

Above: American artillery retreat from Long Island.

The siege of Boston kept British troops trapped in the city for many months. The British government unfairly blamed Gen. Gage for "allowing" the rebellion to get out of hand, and relieved him of command. The new British commander, General Sir William Howe, decided that the only way he could lift the siege was to put his troops on ships and sail away.

The British abandoned Boston in March of 1776. But now they needed to seize another harbor to use as their port. They chose New York Bay and landed about 20,000 troops at Gravesend, Long Island, and at the Verrazano Narrows on August 22, 1776. And so began the Battle of Long Island.

Washington had organized a series of defense lines in what is now the borough of Brooklyn, including a string of strong fortifications at Brooklyn Heights and on nearby hills known as the Heights of Guan. The plan was for the Americans to conduct a fighting retreat from their outlying defenses, inflicting heavy casualties on the British as they went. Once the British troops reached Brooklyn Heights, Washington's cannons would finish them off.

Unfortunately Washington's plan failed. On the morning of August 27, the British, in a diversionary action, blasted away at the front of the American positions. Then, much to their surprise, the Americans heard British cannon fire to their rear! It turned out that during the night, Gen. Howe and 4,000 of his best men, with the help of Loyalists in nearby Queens County, had secretly slipped around the Patriot lines and were now between the Americans and their Brooklyn Heights fortifications. Many of Washington's men panicked and fled.

Washington tried to salvage the situation, but it was impossible. His army was outnumbered two to one, and worse, many of his men were unarmed because they had thrown away their weapons during their retreat. A timely storm on the night of August 29 allowed Washington to safely ferry his troops across the East River. But the British quickly followed and soon forced the American troops completely out of New York City.

They would hold the city until the end of the war.

Battle of
LONG ISLAND
August 27-29, 1776

0 — 4
miles

NEW JERSEY

Hudson River

Manhattan
Island

NEW YORK

Astoria

Flushing
Bay

East River

Flushing

New York City

New Town

WASHINGTON

Brooklyn

Bushwick

Long Island

New York
Bay

Heights of Guan

Bedford

Flatbush

Staten
Island

HOWE

Gravesend

Key

Continental Troops

British Troops

Continental Retreat

British Troop
Movement

British Attack

Continental
Fortifications

City

Road

British Warship

Forest

N

Above: Detail of the firing mechanism of a Hessian flintlock musket.

The late fall of 1776 was not a good time for the colonists. George Washington and his army had been beaten, battered, and chased across New York and into New Jersey. To make matters worse, the enlistment, or term of service, of his small army of less than 6,000 men was slated to end on December 31, leaving him without a fighting force.

In December, Washington wrote in despair to his cousin Lund Washington, "Our only dependence now is upon the Speedy Enlistment of a New Army; if this fails us, I think the game will be pretty well up. . . ."

Washington knew that the best way to raise a new army and to inspire his men to stay in the ranks was a decisive victory against the British, and he had a plan. More than 1,200 Hessians fighting for the British were camped in Trenton, New Jersey. If he could capture or defeat them, it might help inspire more colonists to sign up. Washington also knew that the arrogant Hessians, confident of their superiority over the "inferior" Continental army, would think it safe to celebrate Christmas without posting a strong guard.

A winter storm of rain, hail, and snow that hit the region on December 25 only increased the Hessians' confidence that they had nothing to fear. It was then that Washington struck. On Christmas night, he and his army crossed the Delaware River. In the predawn hours of December 26, he led 2,400 men and 18 cannons on a surprise attack.

The Hessians, drowsy from their late-night Christmas celebrations, were caught completely off-guard. They tried to fight back, but their efforts were scattered and uncoordinated. Within two hours, the Battle of Trenton was over. Washington and his men had won.

Still, if most of his troops failed to reenlist, in five days Washington would find himself a general without an army. Therefore, in an effort to keep his troops together, Washington pledged his personal fortune to pay their salaries if only they would remain. About 1,300 of the 6,000 Continentals agreed to sign up for an additional six weeks. These, together with 3,500 men from a newly arrived Pennsylvanian militia, gave him a viable fighting force. So Washington made plans to follow up his victory at Trenton with an attack on the British garrison at Princeton, several miles away.

Opposite: George Washington crossing the Delaware River.

Quick Facts

In addition to his soldiers, Burgoyne enlisted Native American allies to help him in his campaigns. In one respect, these allies turned out to be worse enemies to him than the American troops. During one of their raids around Saratoga, a band of Native Americans mistakenly killed the Tory Jane McCrea, the fiancée of Lieutenant David Jones, who was a Loyalist who served in Burgoyne's army. News of the atrocity swept the colonies and caused many neutral Americans to rally to the Patriot cause.

Burgoyne had expensive tastes and loved the high life. Even when on a campaign he made sure he lived comfortably. His supplies included fine china, silverware, and gourmet food. He also had a feather bed in his baggage train.

Howe's brother, Admiral Lord Richard Howe, commanded the British fleet in America. Howe owed part of his military advancement to his relationship—by illegitimate descent—to King George III.

Above: Gen. William Howe.

Two of the most celebrated English generals in the early years of the Revolutionary War were Gen. William Howe, the commander in chief of all the British armies in the colonies, and Gen. John Burgoyne, who served under Howe and who eventually became commander of the British army in Canada.

Gen. Howe, of course, was the second British commander in chief, succeeding Gen. Thomas Gage in October 1775. But his appointment did not serve British interests very well. Despite his success in the Battles of Long Island and New York City, he consistently failed to destroy the Continental army when he had the chance. And he had a lazy side. As one German officer who served under him put it, "Sir William liked to enjoy himself, so much so that he sometimes forgot his duties as a commander."

By 1778 he had lost the confidence of the British government, and in turn was replaced by General Sir Henry Clinton.

Gen. Burgoyne had much in common with Howe, but was also a politician and playwright. One of his ambitions was to add a knighthood to his name. He had served with distinction as a soldier in Europe, where he earned the nickname "Gentleman Johnny" for the civil way he treated his troops. But his attitude toward the rebellious Americans was haughty. In one of his speeches to Parliament he said, "I look upon America as our child, which we have already spoilt by too much indulgence."

He didn't think much of American troops either, but his attitude changed during the Battle of Bunker Hill. In a letter to British Prime Minister Lord North, he attempted to describe the enterprising nature of the soldiers he faced, saying, ". . . It may be said of [the Continental army] that every private man will in action be his own general, who will turn every tree and bush into a kind of temporary fortress. . . ."

Even so, Burgoyne remained convinced that the Americans were no match for the British, and, in fact, before he had left for the colonies, had rashly remarked to his friend Charles James Fox that he expected to bring America to its senses before he returned. Fox replied sharply, "I believe when you next return to England you will be a prisoner on parole." And he was right.

Opposite: Burgoyne's surrender to George Washington at Saratoga.

Quick Facts

🔔 In America the year 1777 came to be known as "the Year of the Hangman" because the 7s resembled a gallows used for hanging spies, traitors, and criminals.

🔔 The victories at Trenton and Princeton saved the Revolution for the Americans. Not only did the victories boost the morale of the Patriots, but they also helped the American delegates in France who were trying to get aid and diplomatic recognition from King Louis XVI. After the two victories, the French king agreed to send money, men, supplies, and arms to the Patriots.

🔔 When Washington and his troops crossed the Delaware River, only two men, who had frozen to death, were lost.

Following the victory at Trenton, spirits were high in Washington's Continental army. But Gen. Howe was determined to avenge the British defeat, and ordered General Charles Cornwallis to take his 8,000-man army from New York City, where it was stationed, and attack the American force.

Cornwallis's men fought their way to Trenton on January 2, 1777, capturing the city after a brief, sharp battle. Cornwallis then ordered his men to seize the heights above the town, which they did. A stream and a stone bridge were all that separated the two armies, and the ice-clogged Delaware River was at Washington's back. Cornwallis confidently told his general officers that everything was in place, and that he would take Washington in the morning, as a hunter bags a fox.

But the "fox" had other plans. Washington contrived to slip away with most of his men in the evening, circle around the enemy's rear, and make a quick strike at Princeton. To mask this movement, he had extra campfires set, and left a small group of men behind with orders to make as much noise as possible, even digging fortifications to make it appear that his whole army remained.

On the morning of January 3, 1777, Cornwallis awoke to the sound of artillery fire to his north. At once he realized he had been tricked and that the Continental army was attacking Princeton.

The battle there was a rout. "It is a fine fox chase, my boys!" cried Washington, as if to mock the fox-hunting bugle call which had been sounded by the British during the Battle of Long Island. But as the British troops retreated toward Trenton, Washington chose not to follow, since he knew that his army was too small and too tired to meet Cornwallis's head on. Still, he could be pleased with himself; he had given the Continental army two badly needed victories in a time of near despair.

Above: Washington at the Battle of Princeton.

Opposite: Washington rode on his horse to the front of his troops. "Parade with me my brave fellows," he called to them, before personally leading the assault on the British lines.

Quick Facts

🔔 While there is no proof that Betsy Ross made the American flag, it is known that she *did* make flags for the Pennsylvania navy in 1777.

🔔 Originally, both a star and a stripe were added to the flag whenever a new state was admitted to the Union. During the War of 1812, the Stars and Stripes had fifteen stars and fifteen stripes. But Congress realized that the flag would soon be too big if a new stripe was continually added, so it had the design revised. Only the original thirteen colonies would be represented with a stripe, and all states, existing and newly added, would be represented with a star in the blue field. That is why on today's flag there are fifty stars but only thirteen stripes.

Above: One of the versions of the Stars and Stripes of the American Revolution.

Though their purpose now is largely ceremonial, for many centuries flags served a very practical purpose on the battlefield. Large battle flags—whether national flags or ones belonging to a military unit—were visual reference points to inspire soldiers and to help them locate their lines during the chaos and confusion of close fighting.

American troops and militia carried many different flags during the American Revolution, most with patriotic or defiant slogans written on them. The more popular battle flag themes included a snake or a tree design. The Continental navy flew a bright yellow flag that featured a coiled rattlesnake and the slogan "Don't Tread on Me." The Pine Tree Flag, a white flag with a large green pine tree sewn on it, was popular with New England troops.

The national flag that came to be called the Stars and Stripes was inspired by the design of the Grand Union flag, originally used by Washington's army. The Grand Union flag had a total of thirteen red-and-white stripes, with the British flag in the upper left corner to symbolize the loyalty of many colonials to King George III. But as the Revolutionary War heated up, it became obvious that a change in the flag's design was required.

On June 14, 1777, a brief entry appeared in the journal of Congress: "Resolved that the flag of the U.S. be thirteen stripes, alternate red and white; that the union be thirteen stars, while in a blue field representing a new constellation." This flag was the Stars and Stripes. A circle of thirteen stars in a blue field had replaced the British flag design, which symbolized the complete break that had occurred between the thirteen colonies and the mother country.

No one knows for sure who designed the flag. The most popular legend about its creation involves a seamstress named Betsy Ross. According to the story, George Washington and two other men entered Betsy Ross's Philadelphia shop in June 1776 and hired her to stitch a flag for the new nation based on their design. There is no proof that that ever happened, although the account came from her grandson, William Canby, who told the story to the Pennsylvania Historical Society in 1870. But the story so captivated the popular imagination that generations of people came to believe it was true.

Opposite: The Birth of Old Glory depicts the legend of Betsy Ross.

Quick Facts

In addition to their firearms, many of Col. Friedrich Baum's men had broadswords, an unusual weapon of choice in the American wilderness of the 1770s. Broadswords were long, heavy, and obsolete. Yet, after Baum's men had run out of bullets and gunpowder for their pistols and carbines, they continued the fight with the broadswords, proving that the weapons were not as obsolete as previously thought.

John Stark had fought in the Battle of Bunker Hill. He felt that his heroic actions in that battle had earned him a promotion to brigadier general in the Continental army. When he did not get the promotion, he angrily resigned. Thus, it was as a leader of militia troops (not regular soldiers) that he fought at the Battle of Bennington.

Above: Americans attacking the British at the Battle of Bennington.

In 1777 the key to the British strategy for ending the rebellion was to control the line of the Hudson River and split the colonies in two. Once this happened, the British believed that the Rebels would give up. As part of this strategy Gen. Burgoyne's army began to march south from its Canadian base in June. He expected a welcome from the population of New York and Vermont, which was said to be loyal to the crown. Instead he met hostility, and soon found himself in desperate need of supplies.

When he reached Fort Edward in New York, just south of Lake Champlain, Burgoyne was told that a large quantity of arms and provisions had been stored by the Rebels in nearby Bennington, Vermont. He was also told that it was under a light guard. Burgoyne promptly ordered 800 hand-picked men, led by Colonel Friedrich Baum, to go to seize the cache.

Baum made slow progress through the wilderness because each of his men was heavily burdened with about sixty pounds of supplies, including food, ammunition, and gear. On August 15, they came in contact with a mobile force of about 800 American troops led by Colonel John Stark. Both sides immediately sent for reinforcements.

But Stark was not one to patiently wait for help. Even though the British troops had entrenched themselves on a hill, he was determined to attack and defeat them. "Tonight our flag floats over yonder hill," Stark told his men, "or Molly Stark is a widow!"

Stark's troops surrounded the British position and prepared to attack on August 16. They were skilled woodsmen who knew how to move silently through a forest without being seen, so the British were taken by surprise when they were attacked at dawn. The battle continued all day long until sunset, when the Americans prevailed.

But just at that moment, reinforcements for both sides arrived. Victory might have turned to defeat had not Seth Warner and his Green Mountain Brigade routed the British side. Burgoyne wrote of the Americans he faced in battle: "The New Hampshire Grants [as Vermont was then called], a country unpeopled and almost unknown in the last war, now abounds in the most active and rebellious race on the continent and hangs like a gathering storm on my left."

As news of the victory spread, fresh recruits rushed to join the rebel ranks.

Opposite: The Americans force a British retreat in the Battle of Bennington.

Quick Facts

🔔 John Sullivan was one of Washington's unluckiest generals. It was his misfortune to be in command of the troops who were outflanked, and thus defeated at the Battle of Long Island. He was outflanked in the same manner at Brandywine. After the battle the Continental Congress sought to relieve him of command, but Washington officially acquitted him of any fault.

🔔 At Brandywine, Washington was almost shot by British Major Patrick Ferguson, who later recalled, "I could have lodged half a dozen balls in or about him before he was out of my reach. But it was not pleasant to fire at the back of an unoffending individual who was acquitting himself coolly of his duty, and so I left him alone."

Above: Bullets from the battlefield at Brandywine.

In August 1777, while Burgoyne was slowly making his way south from Canada, British Gen. William Howe landed his own army of 18,000 men at the mouth of Chesapeake Bay. He intended to capture Philadelphia, the Patriots' capital city, which lay just fifty miles away. Gen. George Washington greeted him with an army of 16,000 men.

The center of this force was massed at Chadd's Ford, Pennsylvania, on the east bank of Brandywine Creek, which lay directly across the enemy's line of march.

Early on the morning of September 11, the British attacked. One of their columns, led by the German general Wilhelm von Knyphausen, began to bombard the American position across the creek, as if that were to be the main point of attack. But this was a diversion. The real onslaught would come from British troops led by Gen. Howe and Gen. Cornwallis who were making a flanking movement seventeen miles upstream.

Misled by conflicting reports about their whereabouts, Washington was outmaneuvered, and soon discovered that Cornwallis and his men were at his rear. The British surged across the creek, and captured the American artillery, which was promptly turned against the Continental troops. At the same time, Cornwallis launched a bayonet attack. The American lines broke as the Continentals lost all hope of saving the day. But as they fell back to Chester, Pennsylvania, Washington ordered General Nathanael Greene, who had a force of about 1,500 men, to harass Gen. Howe's pursuing army and delay it long enough for him to plan a new defense.

But Greene was caught off-guard. On the night of September 20, three battalions of British troops with bayonets and swords surprised and attacked his camp. The Americans scattered "in all directions with the greatest confusion," wrote a British officer. "The light infantry bayoneted every man they came up with. The camp was immediately set on fire, and this, with the cries of the wounded, formed altogether one of the most dreadful scenes I ever beheld."

For the Americans, the Battle of Brandywine ended in disaster. Congress was forced to relocate to York, Pennsylvania, as the way to Philadelphia was now wide open to British advance. On September 26, Gen. Cornwallis triumphantly marched in.

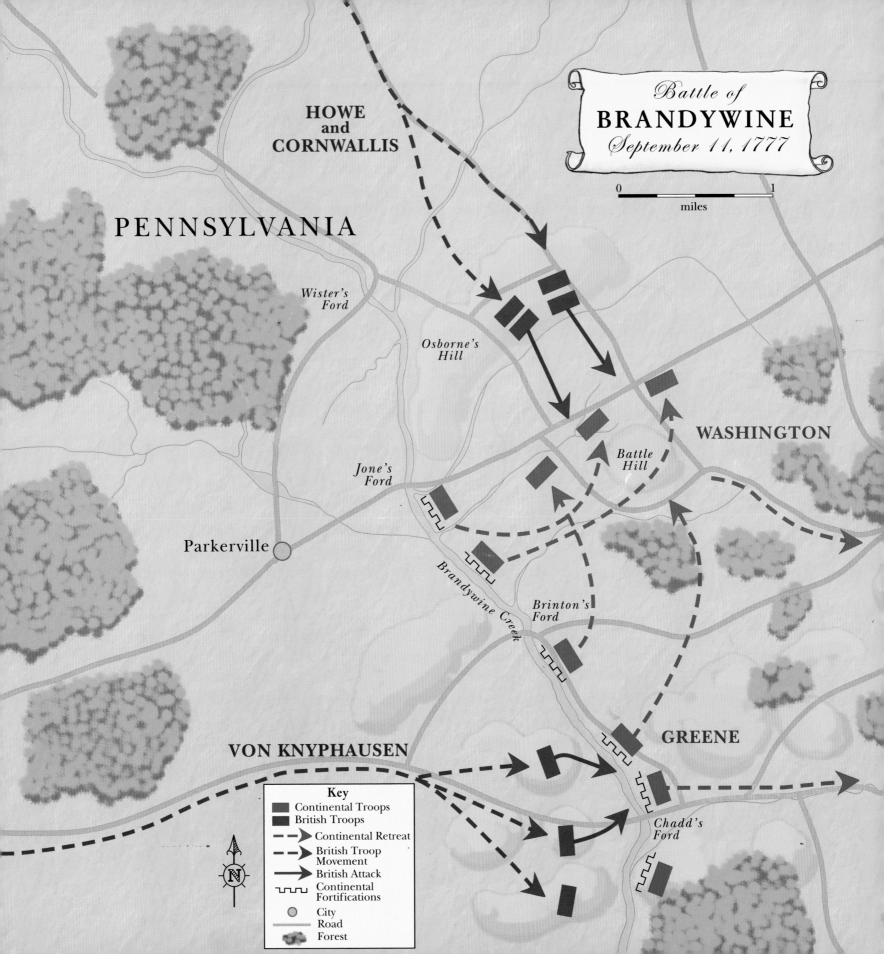

Battle of
BRANDYWINE
September 11, 1777

0 _____ 1
miles

HOWE
and
CORNWALLIS

PENNSYLVANIA

*Wister's
Ford*

*Osborne's
Hill*

WASHINGTON

*Battle
Hill*

*Jone's
Ford*

Parkerville

*Brinton's
Ford*

Brandywine Creek

VON KNYPHAUSEN

GREENE

*Chadd's
Ford*

Key
- Continental Troops
- British Troops
- Continental Retreat
- British Troop Movement
- British Attack
- Continental Fortifications
- City
- Road
- Forest

N

Quick Facts

🔔 One reason for the British setback at Germantown was that their commander, Gen. Howe, had spent the entire night before gambling. When the Americans launched their dawn attack, he was too tired to quickly organize a defense.

🔔 After the war, George Washington lived in Germantown for part of his presidency. Germantown, on higher ground than nearby Philadelphia, was believed to have offered some protection from the yellow fever epidemics that frequently struck the city.

🔔 In a letter to Benjamin Franklin written after the battle, Thomas Paine described the American withdrawal firsthand: "The retreat was extraordinary. Nobody hurried themselves. Everyone marched at his own pace. The Enemy kept a civil distance behind, sending every now and then a Shot after us, and receiving the same from us."

Above: A combination knife and fork used by a soldier at Germantown.

ashington's defense of Philadelphia had thus far been a catastrophe. When the British troops led by Gen. Charles Cornwallis entered the city in September 1777, they wore sparkling parade uniforms and carried polished weapons. The residents clearly understood the message the British general was sending. They couldn't help but be impressed with this demonstration of the might and wealth of the British Empire.

But Washington was determined to undermine the recent British victories. He managed to install enough cannon along the Delaware River to prevent the British fleet from sailing up to reinforce the imperial garrisons in and around Philadelphia. When he learned that Gen. William Howe had dispatched troops to destroy some of his cannon emplacements, Washington seized the opportunity to strike at the British base camp at Germantown, Pennsylvania.

Just after dawn on October 4, 1777, Washington's force of about 11,000 men attacked. The outlying British sentries were driven into the town, and by 9 A.M., the British soldiers were in full retreat.

"The enemy were chased quite through their camp," remembered one soldier. "They left their kettles, in which they were cooking their breakfasts, on the fires; and some of their garments were lying on the ground."

But, in the frenzy of their triumph, Washington's men lost their discipline and became fragmented and disorganized. Then British reinforcements arrived and drove them out.

Though the Battle of Germantown was not a clear-cut American victory, it was certainly not a defeat. Indeed, as George Weedon of Virginia said, "Though the event miscarried, it was worth the undertaking."

Most importantly, in Europe the battle was taken as proof of America's ability to win. As a result, governments in Europe began to take the Revolution more seriously. Some of them even began to consider what sort of aid they might give to the Patriot cause.

Opposite: A romanticized illustration showing the American attack on British troops at Germantown.

Above: Gen. Burgoyne.

he overall British plan, which had Burgoyne marching south from Canada, also called for Gen. William Howe and his men, based in New York City, to move north up the Hudson River to meet Burgoyne and his army halfway. However, Gen. Howe did not get his orders in time to move north. As a result, the Patriot army in New York had only one British army to fight instead of two.

Horatio Gates was commander in chief of the Patriot army in New York. In one skirmish after another, his men skillfully used the shelter of trees and rocks to protect themselves from the British, who had been trained to fight in straight lines and on open ground.

Baroness von Riedesel, who had accompanied her husband, the British Gen. Baron von Riedesel, to the field of battle was trapped in a house not far behind the British lines. "I was full of care and anguish, and shivered at every shot," she wrote afterward, "for I could hear everything. I saw a great number of wounded; and what was still more harrowing, they even brought three of them into the house where I was."

Gen. Burgoyne asked British Gen. Clinton in New York City for reinforcements. But these were sent too late. Burgoyne was trapped at Saratoga in October and forced to surrender to Gen. Gates. Burgoyne stepped up and handed his sword to Gates, simply saying, "The fortune of war, General Gates, has made me your prisoner." The American general instantly returned the sword, replying, "I shall always be ready to testify that it has not been through any fault of your excellency."

As the defeated British troops marched past the Continental army, a Hessian soldier serving in Burgoyne's army noted: "Not one of the Continentals was uniformly clad. . . . Yet no fault could be found in their military appearance, for they stood in an erect and soldierly attitude, and remained so perfectly quiet that we were utterly astounded."

Saratoga was a great victory for the Continental army, but many believed that Gen. Gates was too generous with his terms of surrender. He let Gen. Burgoyne keep all his weapons and ammunition—which the Continental army could have used—and would have allowed all the English soldiers to return to England. Congress, however, refused to honor these terms and kept the redcoats as prisoners of war.

Right: Burgoyne's surrender at Saratoga.

Quick Facts

🔔 Gen. Daniel Morgan hated the British—and with good reason. Years before, during the French and Indian War, he had served under British Gen. Braddock. When he quarrelled with a British officer, he was severely whipped, receiving 499 lashes on his back.

🔔 Morgan's sharpshooters used rifles that were more accurate than smooth-muskets. They could hit a target the size of a man's head at a distance of 250 yards. This was at a time when the standard distance for accurate shooting was approximately fifty yards.

🔔 Daniel Morgan was a cousin of the frontiersman Daniel Boone.

Above: Rangers' Gen. Daniel Morgan.

During the Revolutionary War, British soldiers often faced a style of fighting that was unfamiliar to them. In Europe during the eighteenth century, trained soldiers, all dressed in bright, colorful uniforms, would often line up in large open fields, face one another in organized formations, and proceed to attack according to a set program as signaled by the coded beat of drums. Fighting in America was usually not done according to such plans.

During colonial times, the people had to rely on themselves—not on a standing army of professionals—for their safety. They had to protect their families, for example, against marauding bands of Native American war parties, who were experts in the hit-and-run tactics of guerilla warfare. To survive, the people on the frontier had to learn how to fight in the Native American way, using stealth, camouflage, and quick raids. Those who mastered such tactics were rugged individuals, expert sharpshooters, and skilled woodsmen. And it was this guerilla style of warfare that they would use against the British troops.

Such fighters were called Rangers, after Rogers's Rangers, a group who had fought for the British in the French and Indian War. In the north, the Rangers were led by General Daniel Morgan. In the south, they were led by General Francis Marion—the "Swamp Fox."

Francis Marion and his men fought mostly in South Carolina, and were skilled at such tactics. In fact, the British were forced to adopt a scorched-earth policy that destroyed farms, crops, and livestock in order to prevent such Rangers from living off the land.

Though the fighting in South Carolina was among the most bitter in the war, when the Revolution ended, Marion did not hold on to any hard feelings against those who had remained loyal to the British crown. Instead, he actively campaigned in the South Carolina state assembly to allow Loyalists living in other countries to return as full citizens without any penalty or punishment.

Opposite: A mural of Gen. Francis Marion's encounter with the British.

Above: Washington and Marquis de Lafayette at Valley Forge.

As 1777 drew to a close, the British not only still occupied New York City, but had also captured Philadelphia. Their troops could, therefore, enjoy the comfort of warm winter quarters in both cities. Washington's army, on the other hand, made camp at a strategically important but forlorn place in Pennsylvania called Valley Forge. Though Valley Forge was located between the British troops at Philadelphia and the new headquarters of the Continental Congress at York, Pennsylvania, and was therefore an ideal defensive site, Washington admitted it was "a dreary kind of place and uncomfortably provided."

Washington told his men, "I will share in your hardships and partake of every inconvenience." Not until his soldiers had constructed their own huts did he move himself from a tent into the better shelter of a stone house.

During the four long winter months that the army remained at Valley Forge, many officers' wives, including Martha Washington, came to the camp and did what they could to help. For example, they knitted socks, patched garments, and made shirts.

But conditions in the camp were extremely terrible, partly because the winter was severe but also because the army's supply system had fallen apart. Congress seemed more interested in its own survival than in conducting the business of a nation at war and taking care of the basic needs of the army. Some of the officials in charge of providing for the army were inefficient, incompetent, or corrupt.

Chants of protest could be heard echoing throughout Washington's camp: "No pay! No clothes! No provisions! No rum!" By winter's end, about 2,500 of his men had died of exposure, malnutrition, and disease. Dr. Albigence Waldo of the Continental army noted in his diary, "I am Sick, discontented and out of humor. Poor food, hard lodging—cold weather—Vomit half my time—I can't Endure it—Why are we sent here to starve and freeze?"

Some men went so far as to desertion, but most remained loyal to Washington, if not to the cause. Washington shared their hardships, and his efforts to care for his troops gained their unfaltering respect.

Opposite: Washington with Baron von Stueben at Valley Forge.

Quick Facts

🔔 Both Lafayette and von Steuben served in the Continental army without pay.

🔔 Lafayette was nineteen years old when he was commissioned a major general in the Continental army.

🔔 Even though he swore at the soldiers constantly, Baron von Steuben regarded them with great affection. The soldiers returned this affection—and sometimes got a kick out of his impassioned tirades.

🔔 Baron von Steuben wrote the very first manual for the American army, known as the "blue book." It was so thorough and well-organized that it was used, unchanged, as the standard army manual for many decades.

🔔 One private wrote of Baron von Steuben, "Never before or since have I had such an impression of the ancient fabled God of War as when I looked on the baron."

Above: Maj. Gen. Baron von Stueben.

After the American colonists declared themselves in rebellion, a number of Europeans joined their cause. Some, such as Marie-Joseph-Paul-Yves-Roch-Gilbert du Motier of France, better known in history as the Marquis de Lafayette, and the German Friedrich Wilhelm von Steuben, better known as Baron von Steuben (though he was not really a baron), joined because they believed in the new principles of the republican government Americans had proclaimed in their Declaration of Independence.

Lafayette had been born into a noble family, was trained as a soldier, and had inherited an enormous fortune. He possessed a restless nature, and seemed to find the meaning and purpose he craved for in life, in the American Revolution.

Lafayette distinguished himself at the Battle of Brandywine where he was wounded in the leg. Washington told the doctors who were preparing to treat him, "Take care of him as though he were my son."

Lafayette recovered and continued to serve throughout the war, and was on hand to participate in the defeat of the British during the siege of Yorktown.

Baron von Steuben joined the Continental army at a time of its greatest need. He was a former Prussian officer with battlefield experience, and had been recommended to Washington by Benjamin Franklin. When he arrived at Washington's headquarters in Valley Forge in February 1778, the Continental army was a ragged, dispirited mob. Washington recognized his ability and put him in charge of their training. Though von Steuben spoke only a little English, he soon showed that by uniting Prussian discipline with the independent thinking of the American mind, he could quickly transform the troops into an effective, European-style fighting force.

On March 24, 1778, von Steuben put his newly trained troops through a series of line-and-field maneuvers to show Washington what they could do. Washington was so impressed that on March 28, he appointed von Steuben the inspector general of the army. Congress ratified the appointment less than two months later, and gave him the rank of major general.

Opposite: The Marquis de Lafayette's departure from Mount Vernon.

Quick Facts

🔔 Lord North was a skilled parliamentarian. Once, during a session in the House of Commons, he pretended to doze off while a member of the opposition was arguing against government policy. The orator saw this and complained that the prime minister was asleep. "I wish to God I were," Lord North said in a stage whisper.

🔔 Horace Walpole, the famous English writer and politician, poked fun at Lord North's appearance. He described him as very plain, with "two large prominent eyes that rolled about to no purpose . . . a wide mouth, thick lips, and inflated visage [which] . . . gives him the air of a blind trumpeter."

🔔 During the American Revolution, Great Britain had no written constitution (such as the one we have). In fact it still doesn't. Instead British governments follow a series of charters, customs, traditions, and principles that have accumulated over the years.

Left: Lord North.

The man who led the British government during the Revolutionary War was Prime Minister Frederick Lord North, a rotund, friendly man who had been the boyhood friend of King George III. He came to prominence in Parliament when he was made chancellor of the exchequer (the equivalent of our secretary of the treasury).

In 1769, in order to stop a protest movement in Parliament over his handling of the growing crisis in America, King George III asked his friend to become prime minister to lead the British government. At first Lord North agreed completely with King George III that the Americans had to be brought to heel. When the Townshend duties that were designed to force Americans to pay the expense of keeping British officials in the colonies were under review for repeal by Parliament, he said, "The properest time to exert our right to taxation is when the right is refused. To temporize is to yield. And the authority of the mother country, if it is now unsupported, will be relinquished forever: A total repeal cannot be thought of till America is prostrate at our feet." Not only did he stand firm on the issue of taxing the colonies, but in the wake of the Boston Massacre he also advocated military action and other punishment against Massachusetts. By making an example of Massachusetts, Lord North hoped that the other colonies would back down.

After Gen. Burgoyne's defeat at Saratoga, Lord North learned that a treaty of alliance between France and the rebellious colonies had been signed. That's when he started to question his plan of action. Before the alliance, the war was a "family affair." But with France now in the picture, Britain faced the very real possibility of going to war with one of the great powers of Europe, and that was the last thing Lord North wanted to do. In February 1778, he, in desperation, had Parliament repeal the tea tax and the Coercive Acts, and authorized the dispatch of peace emissaries—the Carlisle Commission—to America to end the rebellion. But his efforts were in vain. Lord North became increasingly discouraged with the progress of the war, and several times tried to resign. But King George III refused to accept his resignation. Lord North would soldier on doing the best he could in an increasingly impossible situation.

Opposite: Cartoon shows a group of men standing to the right, among whom are George Washington, holding the tail of the zebra. Lord North on the left gripping the reins, tries to guide the zebra, whose stripes are the names of the thirteen colonies, onward.

Above: Benjamin Franklin before the lord's council, Whitehall Chapel, London, 1774.

France and Spain were England's rivals in Europe, and had watched with great interest the growing rebellion in America. Both countries had been defeated by England in the past, and saw an opportunity to get their revenge by helping the Americans achieve independence.

France at first was cautious and wanted to see how well the Revolution went. Spain was even more cautious, because it was afraid it would lose its possessions in North America.

In 1778 Congress sent Benjamin Franklin, John Adams, and Arthur Lee to Paris, France, and the court of King Louis XVI. Their mission was a delicate one—to strengthen French support of the American cause, and obtain as much military and economic assistance as possible without sacrificing America's long-term interests.

The cultured and sophisticated world of the French court seduced the provincial American diplomats with its charms. As John Adams wrote to his wife, Abigail: "The delights of France are innumerable. . . . The politeness, the elegance, the softness, the delicacy is extreme. In short, stern and haughty republican as I am, I cannot help loving these people for their earnest desire . . . to please."

Benjamin Franklin, the senior American representative, was well-traveled and Congress had total confidence in him. A brilliant and honest Patriot, possessing keen political instincts and a sharp and subtle wit, Franklin navigated the treacherous corridors of power in the royal court with a style and grace that made him famous and admired throughout the country.

At first France was reluctant to send the Rebels more than token assistance. If the Americans' wavered in their purpose or suffered defeat, France did not want to be in a position of backing a loser. But once King Louis XVI and his ministers saw that Patriot resolve was strong and that victories were being achieved against the British armies, they made their support official. In 1778 a treaty of alliance was signed between America and France, which changed the whole balance of power in the conflict. Americans now rightly believed that victory for their cause was just a matter of time.

Opposite: Reception for Benjamin Franklin in France.

Quick Facts

🔔 For his mishandling of events at Monmouth Courthouse, Lee was court marshaled and removed from service.

🔔 A *poltroon* is a spiritless coward.

🔔 Congress returned to Philadelphia on July 2, 1778, and, two days later, on July 4, many public events were held to celebrate its return.

🔔 As a result of the British occupation of Philadelphia, many homes of prominent Patriots were vandalized. Benjamin Franklin's house was one of those ransacked, with the British carrying off all of his scientific instruments and much of his library.

🔔 Mary Ludwig Hayes, nicknamed "Molly Pitcher" for her service at the Battle of Monmouth Courthouse, where, in addition to helping her husband fire his cannon, she carried water in pitchers for the thirsty soldiers.

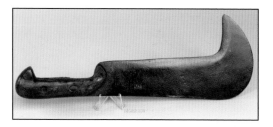

Above: Fascine knife, a common camp tool used to clear brush and other small growth.

en. Sir Henry Clinton became the third commander in chief of the British forces in America in March 1778, replacing Gen. Howe. The British government hoped that Clinton would prove capable of reversing the recent series of British defeats, and quash the revolt. In the summer of that year, Gen. Clinton learned that a French fleet was sailing toward Philadelphia to blockade the mouth of the Delaware River. To avoid being trapped he evacuated Philadelphia in mid-June 1778 and started marching north through New Jersey toward the British base in New York City.

Washington sent a force under the command of General Charles Lee to attack the enemy's rear at the first opportunity. The rest of the Continental army would then rush up to support the attack, if it proved successful. If it was not successful, it would cover Lee's retreat.

On June 28, Lee's troops approached the British rear guard at Monmouth Courthouse in Freehold, New Jersey. The troops under him had been recently trained by Baron von Steuben, and were enthusiastic and eager to fight. Unfortunately for them Lee issued confusing and contradictory orders that created chaos among the units on the field. As a result, the attack was half-hearted. Some troops fought the British while others stood idly by.

Washington was furious, and galloped up to Lee to demand an explanation. Lee, embarrassed, tried to blame the soldiers. "The American troops," he declared, "would not [fight] the British bayonets."

But Washington knew who was really at fault. Angrily he replied, "You . . . poltroon—you never tried them."

Washington then took charge of the battle himself, riding forward into the thick of it, inspiring men who were on the verge of retreating in confusion. His men rallied, reformed their broken ranks, and began fighting again.

As evening fell on the hot, sultry day, the fighting stopped. The next morning the Americans expected to renew the battle where it had left off. But the British had silently retreated during the night toward the harbor of Sandy Hook where they were later picked up by a British fleet.

Because of Lee's poor leadership, the Continental army did not win an outright victory at Monmouth. But American soldiers could proudly say that they held their own against some of the best soldiers in the British army.

Opposite: Mary Ludwig Hayes.

Above: Martha Washington.

*L*ife for women during the American Revolution was very different than it is now. At that time most did not have any formal education. They were not allowed to vote, and any property that they owned was legally controlled by their husbands. Women married early—most were mothers by age thirteen or fourteen, and an unmarried woman of eighteen was considered a spinster.

Despite all this, some women managed to accomplish a great deal, and did far more than take care of their families—though that in itself was a lot! During the war, when their husbands went off to fight, women had to do all the men's work as well as their own. Martha Washington, for instance, managed an 8,000-acre plantation at Mount Vernon. Mary Katherine Goddard became the publisher of her brother's paper the *Maryland Journal and Baltimore Advertiser*. Abigail Adams provided her husband, John Adams, with expert advice on all the major issues of the day. The letters they exchanged constitute an extraordinary record of the American Revolution. Some women also actively participated in the fighting. One such woman was "Molly Pitcher."

"Molly Pitcher" was the nickname of Mary Ludwig Hayes, the wife of an artilleryman in the Continental army. She earned the nickname "Molly Pitcher" for her service at the Battle of Monmouth Courthouse where, heedless of the risk to her life, she helped her husband fire his cannon and carried water in pitchers back and forth from the well for the thirsty troops. One soldier recalled: "While in the act of reaching for a cartridge . . . a cannon from the enemy shot passed directly between her legs, without doing any other damage than carrying away all the lower part of her petticoat. Looking at it with apparent unconcern, she observed that it was lucky it did not pass a little higher . . . and continued [shooting]."

Other women were resourceful in a fix. An example was Temperance "Tempe" Wick, who belonged to a prosperous New Jersey family. In the winter of 1779–80 when the Continental army camped out near the Wick farm, she took her horse and hid it on the second floor of the house when some soldiers came to steal it. The men searched all over but never thought to look upstairs.

Opposite: Nancy Hart captured five British soldiers by getting them drunk and holding them at gunpoint until the militia arrived. Georgia later named a county after her.

Left: Joseph Brant.

Native Americans fought for both sides during the Revolutionary War. Most of the groups were allies of the British who promised that if the British won, they would keep the colonists from taking over Native American lands. The Algonquin, Delaware, and the Iroquois confederations were among the most powerful groups. The Iroquois confederation was also known as the Six Nations, and was made up of the Mohawks, Oneida, Onondaga, Cayuga, Seneca, and Tuscarora groups.

Even though Native Americans were skilled fighters who knew how to move quickly and silently through the wilderness, they were not helpful allies. The warriors were hard to control once the fighting began, and would sometimes attack and kill not only armed soldiers, but also women and children.

During the summer and fall of 1778, the British sponsored Native American raids against frontier colonial settlements. The most savage onslaughts occurred in northern Pennsylvania's Wyoming Valley in July 1778, and later that year in New York's Cherry Valley.

On November 11–12, 1778 a 700-man British force with 500 Native Americans led by Chief Joseph Brant, a Mohawk chief, attacked the Cherry Valley settlements, just fifty miles west of Albany. A reporter from the colonial newspaper the *New Jersey Gazette* later wrote of the massacres:

"The enemy killed, scalped and most barbarously murdered thirty-two inhabitants, chiefly women and children. . . . [They] committed the most inhuman barbarities on most of the dead."

Washington immediately took action to punish the groups that had participated. One of his generals, John Sullivan, led 4,000 men in a month-long campaign in which about 40 Native American settlements were burned. Even the adjacent buildings, orchards, and croplands were destroyed.

Not only did this campaign fail to accomplish what Washington hoped it would; it made the Native Americans even more dependent on the British for their survival.

Opposite: Jane McCrea's brutal murder by a Native American patrol party working with Gen. Burgoyne galvenized colonial militia troops.

Quick Facts

🔔 Gen. Wayne was a bold and dashing general. He was known as "Mad Anthony" Wayne because he could be hotheaded and impetuous in action.

🔔 In 1778 the British tried to negotiate an end to the war. They dispatched the Carlisle Commission, a group of delegates led by Frederick Howard, fifth Earl of Carlisle, to America to try to secure a peace on terms that would have kept the rebellious colonies within the British Empire. All their efforts—including bribery—failed, and they sailed back to England in late November 1778.

🔔 Gen. Wayne is buried in two graves. When he died in 1796, he was buried in Erie, Pennsylvania. Thirteen years later, his son, Isaac Wayne, wanted to have the body moved to the family plot in Radnor, Pennsylvania. Deciding that it was too difficult to take the whole body back, Isaac had Dr. J. Wallace, a veteran who had fought under Gen. Wayne, separate the flesh from his father's bones. Then he had the flesh reburied in Erie and the skeleton buried in Radnor.

The Hudson River was probably the most important waterway in the American Revolution. If the British took control of it, they could divide the colonies in the north from those in the south. If the Continental army held on to it, Washington could prevent British troops from coming south from Canada, and at the same time threaten the British base in New York.

Washington had ordered the construction of two redoubts—temporary defensive fortifications—on the Hudson River. These were Stony Point on the west bank and Verplanck's Point on the east bank, which were created to guard the mountain passes and the key crossing at King's Ferry. When British general Henry Clinton heard of their construction, he attacked and captured them both.

Clinton then orchestrated a series of raids up and down the East Coast in an attempt to lure Washington and his army to open battle. But instead of taking Clinton's bait, Washington developed his own plans for a counter-strike. At length, he decided that Stony Point could be retaken from the British by a surprise attack. General Anthony Wayne was chosen to lead it.

It was a perilous mission. The fort, located on a rocky promontory, was surrounded on three sides by water and joined to the mainland by a causeway extending across a marsh.

On the morning of July 15, 1779, Wayne, with several hundred elite soldiers, got into position. He regarded the assault as suicidal, and wrote to ask a friend to look after his family and to protect his good name after his death. He dated his gloomy letter "15 July 1779, near the hour and scene of carnage."

The troops managed to cross the causeway, and surprise and gag a sentry before he could sound an alarm. So, the British were completely unaware that an attack was in progress until Wayne's men were almost at the fortress walls. Patriots then continued their advance with such speed that they captured the fort in just twenty minutes. The British troops were completely at their mercy. Yet they were spared. Wayne, who had suffered a slight head wound during the assault, proudly wrote to Washington, "The humanity of our brave soldiery who scorned to take the lives of a vanquished foe . . . reflects the highest honor on them and accounts for the few of the enemy killed."

Opposite: The storming of Stony Point.

Quick Facts

🔔 The *Bonhomme Richard* was originally designed as a cargo ship, not a warship. As a result, it was much slower than regular warships such as the *Serapis*. It is a credit to Jones's skills as a captain that he was able to overcome his own ship's deficiencies and defeat the enemy.

🔔 After the Revolution, John Paul Jones served in the Russian navy of Catherine the Great.

🔔 Jones died in France in 1792. His remains were not returned to the United States until 1905, when they were entombed in 1913 at the U.S. Naval Academy in Annapolis, Maryland.

Above: John Paul Jones.
Opposite: Bonhomme Richard vs. HMS *Serapis.*

No naval career during the American Revolution was more celebrated than that of John Paul Jones. Born in Scotland, Jones had come to America as a cabin boy on a merchant ship. When the Revolutionary War broke out, he was commissioned as a first lieutenant in the Continental navy, and he quickly established himself as a bold captain and a dangerous foe.

Abigail Adams, who knew Jones well, wrote: "From the intrepid character he justly supported in the American navy, I expected to have seen a rough, stout, warlike Roman. . . . [But] he is small of stature, well proportioned, soft in his speech, easy in his address, polite in his manners, vastly civil. . . . He is said to be a man of gallantry and a favorite amongst the French ladies. . . ."

In August 1779 Jones took command of the *Bonhomme Richard*, a French warship with forty cannons that had been named in honor of Benjamin Franklin's *Poor Richard's Almanac*. Together with a fleet of four ships, he raided towns and cities along the British coast, captured merchant ships, and sold their cargos to buy needed weapons and supplies for the Patriots' cause. He even managed to sail part way up the mouth of the Thames River. Great Britain had already experienced isolated raids by American ships. But the extraordinary extent of Jones's piratical attacks threw the British people along the coast into a panic, and they appealed to King George III for protection. That protection came in the form of the HMS *Serapis*, a new and powerful frigate of fifty cannons commanded by Captain Richard Pearson. On September 23, 1779, the *Serapis* and the *Bonhomme Richard* clashed in a tremendous duel on the high seas. Jones later wrote: "The battle . . . was continued with Unremitting fury. Every method was practiced on both sides to gain an advantage and rake each other; and I must confess that the enemy's ship, being much more manageable than the *Richard*, gained thereby several times an advantageous situation in spite of my best endeavors to prevent it."

Eventually the two ships collided and were literally locked together, deck to deck. Capt. Pearson, thinking that Jones was ready to surrender, called out to him, "Has your ship struck?" Defiantly Jones replied, "I have not yet begun to fight!" His determination carried the day. Even though both ships were severely damaged, it was Pearson who surrendered and offered Jones his sword.

Above: Count Casimir Pulaski.

Savannah, Georgia, on the border of South Carolina, was an important seaport and the capital of the colony of Georgia during the Revolutionary War. In the fall of 1778 Gen. Sir Henry Clinton sent 3,500 British troops under the command of Brigadier General Archibald Campbell to try to take the town from the Patriots. At a cost of only three men killed and ten wounded, the British defeated the Rebels with embarrassing swiftness, and captured the port. Then they used Savannah as a base of operations for their advance through Georgia and the Carolinas. However, they failed in their attempt to capture Charleston, South Carolina, in the summer of 1779 and retreated to their Savannah base.

The Americans were eager to follow up on their victory at Charleston by taking back Savannah. A colonial army led by General Benjamin Lincoln, with the help of a French fleet led by Admiral Charles Hector, the comte d'Estaing, surrounded the city. On October 3, 1779, the siege of Savannah began.

The comte d'Estaing wanted Lincoln and Lincoln's subordinate, Brigadier General Casimir Pulaski, and their men to move quickly and attack. But Lincoln advised against it. The British were cut off by land and sea, and eventual victory for the French and Americans seemed assured. D'Estaing insisted the assault go forward and even threatened to abandon the siege entirely if the Americans did not cooperate. Lincoln went along.

Just before daybreak on October 9, the Patriots began their ill-advised attack. They counted on surprise, but with the help of local spies, the British had learned of their movements in advance and were awake and ready. The battle was sharp, bitter, and bloody. Many Patriots fell. Count Pulaski was notable for his bravery, and repeatedly led his cavalry in a futile attempt to charge through a breach in the British lines. By the time the battle was over, Pulaski was mortally wounded and some 1,000 French and American troops lay dead. The comte d'Estaing himself was among the wounded. The British had lost only 150 men.

Though the siege continued for a few more days it ended in defeat on October 18. With it all hope was lost for a quick American victory in the south. An angry and humiliated d'Estaing took his fleet back to a French colonial port in the West Indies. Lincoln withdrew to Charleston, which he now had to fortify against British attack.

Opposite: Count Pulaski being shot during the Battle for Savannah.

Quick Facts

🔔 Clinton had participated in the Battle of Bunker Hill at the beginning of the Revolutionary War. At the time, the determination of the American militia impressed him. He later wrote in his diary that the battle was "a dear-bought victory; another such would have ruined us."

🔔 In 1786 the British government made Cornwallis governor general of India where he was responsible for reorganizing its administration. He was brilliant at it and his success there is one reason why India remained a part of the British Empire until 1947.

Right: Sir Henry Clinton
Below: Gen. Charles Cornwallis

Gen. Sir Henry Clinton and Gen. Charles Cornwallis were the most important British generals in the latter years of the war. Unfortunately for the British, the two men despised each other and their disagreement over strategy escalated into a severe and venomous dispute. Their inability to get along would contribute to Britain's defeat.

As already pointed out, Clinton had succeeded Gen. Howe as the British commander. Interestingly enough, Clinton had grown up in New York where his father had been a royal governor. Then he had served in the British army in Europe, rising to the rank of major general before being posted to Boston in 1775. After the Battle of Bunker Hill he was promoted to lieutenant general. For the great skill he showed in the Battle of Long Island, he was knighted by King George III.

Putting his personal feelings aside, Clinton knew that Cornwallis was a good general. That was why he gave him command of the British army in the South. There Cornwallis had a number of victories and came close to outright success on that front. But Cornwallis tended to underrate the generals of the Continental army. In particular he scornfully called Lafayette "the boy."

Clinton, a less haughty man, was cultivated and musical and sponsored concerts and plays while his troops occupied New York City. But Benjamin Franklin's son, William, who was a Loyalist, also observed of him that though "gallant to a proverb and possessing great military knowledge in the field," Clinton was "weak, irresolute, unsteady, vain, incapable of forming any plan himself, and . . . too proud and conceited to follow that of another." Because of his fear that Washington would attack New York City, Clinton kept all his troops with him, refusing to send desperately needed reinforcements to Cornwallis at Yorktown, thus contributing to Cornwallis's momentous defeat.

After the American Revolution, Clinton and Cornwallis would carry on their feud in England, blaming each other for how the war turned out. Ultimately, most came to feel that the fault could not be laid at Cornwallis's feet.

Opposite: This cartoon shows America as a snake, with two of three coils around troops commanded by Burgoyne and Cornwallis at the time of their surrender.

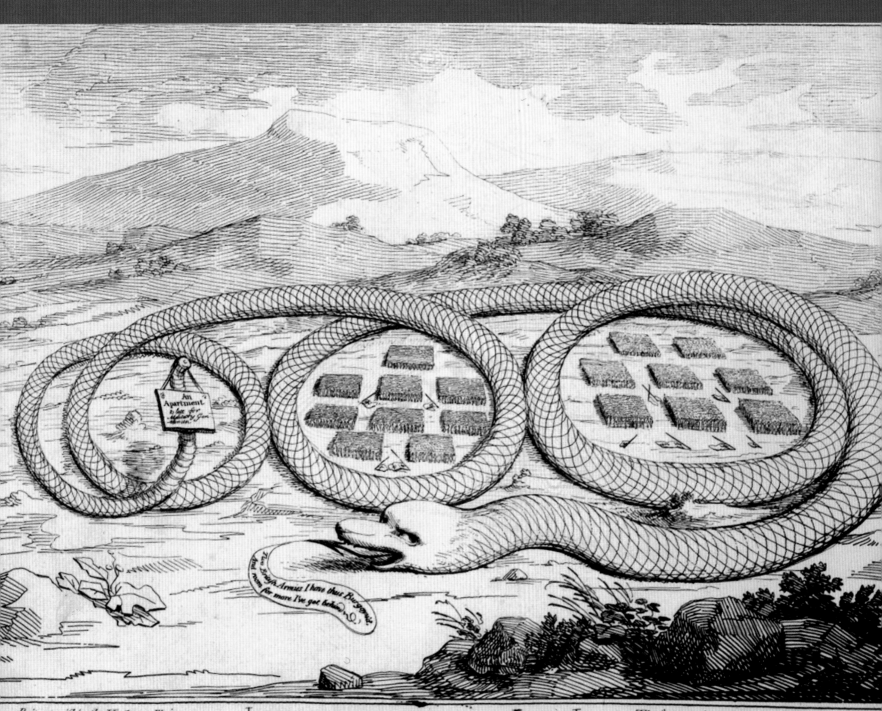

Britons within the Yankeean Plains,
Mind how ye March & Trench,

The AMERICAN RATTLE SNAKE.

The Serpent in the Congress reigns,
As well as in the French.

Pub.d April 12th 1782. by W. Humphrey, N.o 227 Strand.

Quick Facts

⚑ Banastre Tarleton was described as being coldhearted, vindictive, and utterly ruthless. His "total war" tactics of destroying frontier settlements and farms and putting even innocent civilians to the sword made him the most hated man in the south. After the war, he left the army and entered politics, becoming a member of Parliament.

⚑ Unlike the regular British troops who wore red coats, Tarleton's unit wore green to blend in with the landscape.

⚑ *The Brave Boy of the Waxhaws* shows Andrew Jackson, who later became president, as a boy of thirteen. He enlisted in the army, and in 1780 was taken prisoner by the British. When Jackson was ordered by an officer to clean his boots, he indignantly refused, and received a sword cut for this temerity.

Above: Lt. Banastre Tarleton.

In April of 1780, a contingent of 350 Virginia Patriots led by Colonel Abraham Buford hurried toward Charleston, South Carolina, where they hoped to help the Americans under siege. Unfortunately they were unable to reach the city before its surrender in the siege of Charleston in early May, when the 5,400-man garrison, along with four ships and a military arsenal, fell into British hands. It was probably the worst Patriot defeat so far in the war.

Meanwhile Col. Buford and his men made their escape northward, until they came to Waxhaw, a picturesque village near the North Carolina border. There they were overtaken by British Lieutenant Banastre Tarleton who commanded a force of Tories known as Tarleton's Legion. On the afternoon of May 29, Buford's men were making their way through a sparse wood when the British, yelling like banshees, suddenly attacked. The Virginians fought back valiantly but soon saw that further resistance was hopeless and, as an American doctor who was with them recalled, "ordered a flag to be hoisted and the arms to be grounded, expecting the usual treatment sanctioned by civilized warfare." But Tarleton was in no mood to abide by the rules.

Instead he ordered his men to fix their bayonets and advance without mercy against the now defenseless men. "[F]or fifteen minutes after every man was prostrate," wrote the horrified doctor, "[the British] went over the ground, plunging their bayonets into everyone that exhibited any signs of life."

Charles Stedman, a British officer, wrote: "One hundred and thirteen were killed on the spot, and . . . one hundred and fifty were badly wounded. . . .The King's troops were entitled to great commendation for their activity and ardour . . . but the virtue of humanity was totally forgot."

Many Patriots would remember this atrocity and would exact their own revenge later at the Battle of Kings Mountain.

Opposite: The Currier and Ives print entitled
The Brave Boy of the Waxhaws.

Above: Gen. Horatio Gates.

Two of George Washington's most important generals were Horatio Gates and Nathanael Greene. Gen. Gates was a native-born Englishman who embraced the Revolution, and became a leading figure in the Continental army. He seemed well-qualified for any command. He had been educated in Britain's military academies, had shown a gift for organization, and had a wide-ranging knowledge of military affairs. He also had a knack for getting along with others, and after Congress appointed him adjutant general, he did much to help get the Continental army into shape.

He reached the zenith of his fame and popularity when he defeated Gen. John Burgoyne and his British army in the Battle of Saratoga. But soon after that, his reputation was damaged by the charge (later proved false) that he had plotted to undermine George Washington's authority to make himself commander in chief. His reputation really plummeted after his appointment as head of the Continental army in the South where his service would end in disgrace.

Washington had never been sure of Gates's loyalty. On the other hand, he had complete confidence in Nathanael Greene. Greene was self-taught in the science and art of war. But his great intelligence, leadership skills, and ability to admit to and learn from his mistakes made him an outstanding commander. Washington thought so much of him that in 1778 he made him quartermaster general—the man responsible for getting an army all the weapons and supplies, including food, tents, and clothing, that it needs. Greene attacked the huge problems facing him with such energy and dedication that he succeeded where others had failed.

His concern extended to veterans as well. In one of many letters to John Adams on the subject, he urged him "to press upon Congress the necessity of providing pensions for soldiers who were wounded or incapacitated. [This would be] the most effective possible recruiting measure, as even a zealous patriot would hesitate to enlist if he thought a disabling wound might make him a pauper and impoverish his family."

Opposite: Gen. Nathanael Greene.

Quick Facts

🔔 Gates compounded the misery of his men on the march when he gave them a ration of molasses as a treat instead of rum. The molasses, combined with an almost indigestible diet of raw foods, caused crippling diarrhea in the ranks.

🔔 Gen. George Washington had wanted Gen. Nathanael Greene to lead the Patriot armies in the south. But Congress over-ruled him, as Gates was then known as the hero of the Battle of Saratoga, and it was thought his reputation as a winner would lift the morale of the southern troops.

Above: When one colonel told Gen. Gates "We have Cornwallis against us!" Gates confidently replied, "He will not dare to look me in the face."

After the British captured Charleston, South Carolina, in May 1780, Lord Cornwallis undertook to extend British control throughout the south. He planned an elaborate campaign that would take him through both South and North Carolina and into Virginia.

Congress decided Gen. Horatio Gates was the right man to face him and, on June 13, 1780, made Gates the supreme commander of the American forces in the south. When Gates arrived at his new headquarters, he shocked the troops—who were poorly organized, demoralized, and ill—when he decided to go on the offensive at once. His object was Camden, South Carolina, which was in British hands. Almost all of his subordinate officers protested, especially after he opted to march through a wilderness of pine barrens, making it impossible for the army to get supplies. Gates, however, assured everyone that these were on their way.

The march itself was a disaster. Disease, hunger, and a terrible summer heat steadily thinned the ranks. In desperation men drank water from puddles on the ground and ate unripened corn and peaches still half green. What's more, the promised supplies never came.

Even so, on August 15, the faltering Continental army moved into position to attack. That night, scouts from both camps ran into each other in the dark.

At daybreak the Battle of Camden began on a narrow stretch of ground with swamps on either side. As soon as the two armies engaged, Gates's men threw down their weapons, and fled without firing a shot. It was one of the most appalling moments of the war.

Gates later claimed that he had tried to stop the rout, but evidence is against this. Apparently he "chased" his men on horseback—and did not stop until he reached Charlotte, North Carolina, sixty miles away—ahead of his scattered army! Alexander Hamilton gave voice to the general disgust when he remarked, "Was there ever such an instance of a general running away . . . from his whole army?" A court of inquiry looked into Gates's conduct, and on October 14, 1780, he was replaced by Gen. Nathanael Greene.

In the south, Greene rescued what appeared to be a hopeless situation for the Americans, and eventually turned the tide. In fact Greene's brilliant tactics laid the foundation for Cornwallis's ultimate defeat at Yorktown.

Opposite: The Battle of Camden.

Above: Painting entitled *Death to John André.*

Though Benedict Arnold would rise to the rank of major general in the Continental army, he never seemed satisfied. Brilliant, daring, and a good leader of men, he was also vain, arrogant, sensitive to criticism, enjoyed expensive living, and as Patriot Aaron Burr noted, "utterly unprincipled and has no love of country or self-respect to guide him. He is not to be trusted anywhere but under the eye of a superior."

Yet Washington, the commander in chief of the Continental army, did trust him for a time. Arnold was a hero; his bravery on the battlefield had been proven many times, at Ticonderoga, Saratoga, and elsewhere. But his character kept him in the midst of controversy. Thoughts of treason apparently first entered his head in April 1779, when Congress recommended that he be court-martialed for misconduct and abuse of power. In particular, he was charged with embezzling government money for personal use while he was military governor of Philadelphia. Arnold felt that the government for which, in his own mind, he had sacrificed so much, just didn't appreciate his services. On top of that, he had a new young wife who was a British sympathizer and many wealthy associates who were loyal to the British crown. At length, his increasing disenchantment led him to secretly contact the British and offer his services to them for pay. He wanted a lot of money, and the British were eager to make a deal.

In the summer of 1780, Arnold was appointed commandant of the strategic fortress on the Hudson River at West Point. Whoever possessed it would control the river. Arnold devised a plan in collaboration with Major John André, a master British spy, to surrender the fort to the British. But, just in the nick of time, André was captured. The documents he had received from Arnold were discovered and Arnold's treachery was made plain. Then Arnold became aware of his own danger and effected a hair-raising escape to British lines.

On September 26, Gen. Nathanael Greene announced to the army, "Treason of the blackest dye was yesterday discovered. General Arnold, who commanded at West Point . . . was about to deliver up that important post into the hands of the enemy. . . ." Most could scarcely believe their ears.

Opposite: This painting shows Arnold audaciously leading troops into Canada in 1775.

Quick Facts

🔔 The British and Tories suffered some 400 casualties in the battle, including 157 killed. Ferguson was among the slain.

🔔 Six days before his death, Ferguson wrote a rallying letter to his troops: "If you choose to be degraded for ever and ever by a set of mongrels, say so at once, and let your women turn their backs upon you, and look out for real men to protect them."

🔔 The supply situation for the army of Cornwallis in the south grew steadily worse. Even though he received some supplies from England, his army depended on what his foraging parties—small groups of armed soldiers sent out to obtain food from local sources—could find. These foraging parties came under increasing attack by Patriots as the tide of war turned.

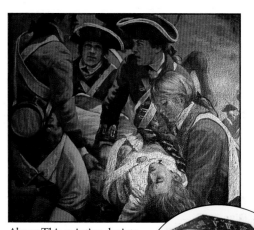

Above: This painting depicts Ferguson's death during the Battle of King's Mountain. *Right:* The compass was an essential tool for navigating the wilds of America.

After British Gen. Cornwallis defeated Gen. Gates at the Battle of Camden, he sent Major Patrick Ferguson with 200 British troops to the western part of the state to establish a training camp for Tory troops. By June, Ferguson had a substantial force under his command. He then marched his Tory battalion on a fighting and recruiting expedition through western North Carolina. Ferguson was a smart commander—tough but fair to his men. He was also a marksman of almost supernatural skill. The Patriots were convinced they had to stop him or risk losing both the Carolinas and Georgia.

On October 6, 1780, Ferguson came to Kings Mountain on the border between North and South Carolina, where a Patriot force had been gathering against him. He was therefore compelled to make a stand.

Kings Mountain, rising sixty feet above the countryside, is more a large hill than a mountain but Ferguson had positioned his men and drawn all his supply wagons together to reinforce the most exposed point of his line. He had only about 1,100 men with him, but his position seemed invincibly strong.

A motley Patriot troop of about 1,400 men arrived the following day. Most were "over-mountain men" as they were called, and wild frontiersmen. They had traveled for thirty-six hours without rest, and some had not eaten for two days. Even so, they were spoiling for a fight.

Ferguson's men were arrayed across the top of the hill, but the thick forest cover of the wooded slopes protected the Patriots as they advanced. It also enabled them to engage in the sniper and guerilla warfare tactics they knew best. Yard by yard they fought their way to the crest but twice failed to take it in a charge. But on the third try, they succeeded. At that point, Ferguson's men began to cry for quarter—wanting to surrender. But it took some time for the fighting to end as some of the Patriots shouted, "Tarleton's quarter!"—meaning no surrender should be accepted, in recollection of the massacre at Waxhaw.

The Battle of Kings Mountain shattered Cornwallis's left flank and marked the beginning of the end of British hopes for the war.

Opposite: Maj. Patrick Ferguson.

Above: British attack at Cowpens

On January 13, 1781, the Patriot general Daniel Morgan received a message from Gen. Greene: "Colonel Tarleton is said to be on his way to pay you a visit. I doubt not but he will have a decent reception and proper dismission."

Morgan immediately began looking for a place where he could meet Tarleton on adventageous ground. The site he picked was called "the Cowpens," named for a large stockyard, with the Broad River at his back.

Morgan had militia as well as Continental soldiers under his command, but he knew the militia were unreliable and would almost certainly panic and run the minute the British attacked. So, cleverly, he put them on the front lines and told them not to worry about holding their ground! Instead he told them to stand firm just long enough to fire at the British three times—which was sure to do some damage—then run off to the left to get behind the Continentals as fast as they could. Morgan figured the British would mistakenly think the Patriots were fleeing and so surge forward—straight into his cavalry and regular troops!

The night before the battle, wrote an American soldier, Morgan "went among the volunteers, helped them fix their swords, joked with them about their sweethearts, told them to keep in good spirits, and the day would be ours. . . ."

"'Just hold up your heads, boys, three fires,' he would say, 'and you are free, and then when you return to your homes, how the old folks will bless you, and the girls will kiss you for your gallant conduct!'"

The Battle of Cowpens began on January 17, 1781. Tarleton attacked at dawn. Morgan's militia fired three times and ran back as instructed. Scenting victory, the British charged and, just as Morgan had predicted, ran headlong into the stalwart heart of the American force. The Americans stood their ground, fired, and then advanced with their bayonets fixed.

At the same time, cavalry under Col. William Washington, cousin to George Washington, also attacked, descending on the British like a whirlwind. The shock was so sudden and violent that Tarleton's troops were overwhelmed.

According to Patriot general William Moultrie, who heard about the battle while being held at Charleston as a prisoner of war, "This defeat . . . chagrined and disappointed the British officers and Tories exceedingly. . . .This great victory . . . changed the face of American affairs."

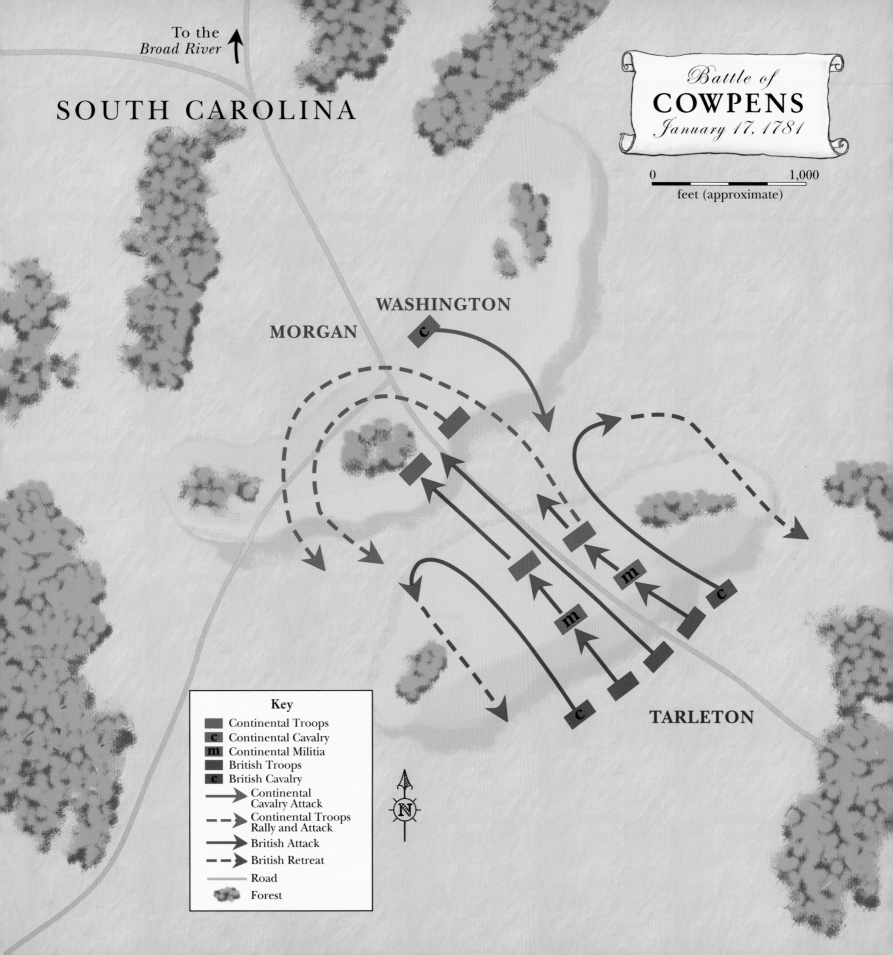

To the
Broad River

SOUTH CAROLINA

Battle of
COWPENS
January 17, 1781

0   1,000
feet (approximate)

MORGAN

WASHINGTON

c

m

m

c

m

m

c

TARLETON

Key
■ Continental Troops
c Continental Cavalry
m Continental Militia
■ British Troops
c British Cavalry
→ Continental
   Cavalry Attack
--→ Continental Troops
   Rally and Attack
→ British Attack
--→ British Retreat
— Road
🌳 Forest

N

Quick Facts

⚲ Remarkably enough, Gen. Greene wrested control of the south from the British without ever winning a major battle. "We fight, get beat, rise and fight again," he said. It was this strategy that steadily eroded Loyalist morale and British military strength.

⚲ Nathanael Greene is regarded by most historians as the second greatest general in the Continental army after George Washington. He had an ironic nickname, "Fighting Quaker" (the Quakers, a religious sect, are usually pacifists).

⚲ A month before the Battle of Yorktown, Lieutenant Benjamin Gilbert wrote to his father, "Nothing but the warmest Expectations of capturing Cornwallis keeps my spirits high, my Cloths beings almost worne out, and no money to get new ones, having Received but 25 Dollars since March Eighty . . . and no expectations of getting any soon."

Above: Nathanael Greene, whose motto was "We fight, get beat, rise, and fight again," was awarded this medal after the battle of Eutaw Springs.

organ's victory at Cowpens was almost an exception for the Continentals in the south. But even though the British won most of the battles, in reality they gained nothing by them for each encounter wore down their troops. Soon the British did not have enough men to control the territory they had seized and still keep on the attack. This was due to the brilliant strategy of Gen. Nathanael Greene, and it earned the grudging respect of his chief adversary, Gen. Cornwallis, who noted, "He is as dangerous as Washington. He is vigilant, enterprising, and full of resources—there is little hope of gaining any advantage over him. I never feel secure when encamped in his neighbourhood."

The British army's last stand in the Carolinas came on September 8, 1781, at Eutaw Springs, South Carolina. After four hours of hard fighting, the British were forced to retreat—losing almost half of their men. But just when total victory was at hand, the American troops foolishly stopped to loot the British camp. A quick British counterattack drove the Americans away. What should have been a decisive American victory ended in a draw. Yet it is hard to blame the Americans for being distracted. As one American colonel wrote afterward, "The [British] tents were all standing and presented many objects to tempt a thirsty, naked, and fatigued soldiery."

In fact many American troops fought almost in rags because Congress did not have the money to provide them with uniforms. Gen. Greene was only exaggerating slightly when he confessed, "At the battle of Eutaw Springs, hundreds of my men were naked as they were born. The bare loins of many were galled by their cartridge-boxes, while a folded rag or a tuft of moss alone protected their shoulders from being chafed by their guns."

Cornwallis would continue his retreat north, not stopping until he reached the Virginia city of Yorktown where he would face his demise.

Opposite: Engraving entitled *The Provision Train.*

Quick Facts

🔔 Late in the war when the army was approaching Yorktown, Gen. Charles Cornwallis ordered Col. Tarleton to try to capture Virginia governor Thomas Jefferson, then living in Charlottesville. Thanks to a timely warning, Jefferson escaped—just three hours in advance of Tarleton's men.

🔔 The decisive impact of the victory at Yorktown was not immediately apparent to Washington. British troops still held New York City and a number of other major cities. He thought there would be another year's worth of fighting.

Above: Lieutenant Colonel Tilghman of Washington's staff announces the surrender of Cornwallis on the steps of Independence Hall in Philadelphia.

On September 28, 1781, the battle that decided the outcome of the American Revolution, the siege of Yorktown, Virginia, began. Cornwallis had retreated to this port city, built fortifications for its defense, and waited for reinforcements.

But Gen. George Washington was confident of a Continental victory. Recently a French fleet under the command of comte de Grasse had arrived with supplies, weapons, and troops. This allied force had harried Cornwallis's army as it moved toward Yorktown. Now it was time for the decisive battle to begin.

Baron von Steuben observed in a letter to Gen. Greene, "Cornwallis is fortifying himself like a brave general who must fall." The combined American and French forces numbered 16,000 men. The British defenders were approximately 7,500. The British entrenchments were strong enough to withstand an attack, but they could not weather a lengthy siege.

While the American and French troops closed in by land, Comte de Grasse's fleet sealed off Yorktown Harbor to prevent the arrival of any British reinforcements by sea.

Washington's men advanced into the outer ring of defense works, which the British then hastily (and unnecessarily) abandoned.

On the night of October 16, Cornwallis attempted to escape across the York River, but a storm arose, forcing him back. After a siege of thirteen days, on October 17—the anniversary of Burgoyne's capitulation at Saratoga—Cornwallis signaled his desire to surrender. On October 19 his troops became American prisoners of war.

Cornwallis was so embarrassed by his defeat that he refused to take part in the ceremony himself. Instead, he had his aide, Brigadier General Charles O'Hara, officially surrender for him. O'Hara, in fact, tried to surrender to the comte de Rochambeau, a French general, who politely pointed to Washington. Washington, in response, had one of his own subordinates, Gen. Benjamin Lincoln, accept the surrender on his behalf.

After he received news of the surrender, Lord North saw that the end had come. He cried out in despair, "Oh, God! Oh, God! It is over! It is over!" All that Britain could do now was negotiate a peace treaty on acceptable terms.

Opposite: A romanticized Currier and Ives print showing how the surrender of Cornwallis at Yorktown *should* have occurred.

SURRENDER OF CORNWALLIS,
AT YORK-TOWN Va. OCT. 1781.

Right: A page of the Treaty of Paris that shows the official government seals.

As its authorized representatives, Congress sent John Jay, John Adams, and Benjamin Franklin to Paris to negotiate a peace treaty with Great Britain that would recognize American independence. The trio were also to consult with French King Louis XVI and his ministers about the terms of the treaty as the French had given the Americans so much help during the war.

But the French were not necessarily looking out for America's best interests. They planned to use the Americans as pawns in their power game with Great Britain and tried to engineer a settlement that would have obliged the new United States to remain somewhat dependent on France.

Jay, Adams, and Franklin recognized the situation they were in. They refused to be sidetracked from their goal, or to be drawn into any agreement that threatened to weaken America's position in international affairs. Despite their relative lack of experience, they bested the most sophisticated diplomatic minds in Europe.

On September 3, 1783, Jay, Adams, and Franklin signed the Treaty of Paris, the agreement that ended the war and gave full diplomatic recognition to the United States of America. Congress officially ratified it on January 14, 1784. It was an extraordinary document for it also redrew the map of North America.

Under the terms of the treaty, Britain agreed to new borders for the United States, including all land from the Great Lakes on the north to Florida on the south, and from the Atlantic Ocean to the Mississippi River. Britain also agreed to remove all of its troops from America. At the same time, the United States would allow British troops that were still in America to return to England. America agreed to pay all existing debts owed to Britain, and also agreed not to persecute Loyalists still in America, but allow those that left the country to return.

After the preliminary Treaty of Paris was signed, a French diplomat remarked that the United States would become "the greatest empire in the world," which was a swipe at the British empire. "Yes sir," replied his British counterpart, "and they will *all* speak English, every one of 'em."

At long last, the war was over. The real work of building a new nation could begin.

Opposite: Independence is declared!

Hamilton delin.

Noble sculp.

The Manner *in which the* American Colonies *Declared themselves*
INDEPENDANT *of the* King *of* ENGLAND,
throughout the different Provinces, on July 4. 1776.

Above: The marriage of George and Martha Washington.

The early years of the United States were full of turmoil. At first Congress tried to govern through a charter called the Articles of Confederation, adopted in 1781. But the charter gave Congress inadequate authority. Most of the real power still belonged to the individual states, which were governed by their own laws.

Chaos threatened to develop. So it was decided to form a stronger central government. After much debate at a national Constitutional convention that met in Philadelphia, the American Constitution—one of the greatest documents in political history—was born. Overall it gave more power to the federal government, and established three separate branches of government—executive, legislative, and judicial.

Washington, one of the delegates, wrote about the Constitution to Lafayette, who was by then back in France, "It is the result of four months' deliberation. . . . If it be good, I suppose it will work its way; if bad, it will recoil on the framers." No one was sure how it would all work out.

In 1789, after the new Constitution had been ratified, the electoral college, which had the responsibility of electing the president of the United States, unanimously chose George Washington to be the first president.

On the eve of his election Washington confided to his friend, General Henry Knox, that he was accepting the office with great misgiving and reluctance. He foresaw "an ocean of difficulties" ahead for which he believed he lacked the necessary political skill. "Integrity and firmness are all I can promise," he concluded. "These, be the voyage long or short, shall never forsake me, although I may be deserted by all men."

The first capital of the United States of America was New York City. On April 30, 1789, Washington was sworn in at a ceremony that took place on Wall Street. The large crowd that witnessed the event was jubilant—and their joy was reflected in celebrations throughout the country. The only person not celebrating was Washington himself. "I greatly fear that my countrymen will expect too much from me," he said to a friend.

But Washington's fears about his own qualifications turned out to be unfounded. He proved to be a great president, and his firm guidance of the nation through two terms of office established a solid foundation for the new republic at the beginning of its life.

Opposite: Inauguration of George Washington.

Glossary

Adjutant general—A general who is responsible for the orderly administration of the army.

Ambassador—The highest-ranking diplomatic representative of one country who is sent to another country.

Ammunition—Projectiles that are fired from weapons such as pistols, rifles, muskets, and cannons. These include bullets, cannon shells, and rockets.

Arsenal—A place used to make and store weapons and ammunition.

Artillery—Weapons, such as cannons and mortars, that discharge ammunition.

Assault—A military attack upon an enemy position.

Barracks—A group of buildings used to house soldiers.

Bayonet—A knife attached to the muzzle end of a rifle, and used in close combat.

Blockade—The isolation of an area or region by a warring nation to prevent anyone or anything from going in or out.

Brigadier general—An officer of the army who commands a brigade.

Campaign—A series of military operations undertaken to achieve a specific goal in a war.

Cavalry—Combat troops mounted on horses.

Civilian—Any person who is not in the military.

Colony—A territory distant from the country that rules it.

Conservative—A person who wishes to preserve traditions or institutions, and who resists change.

Diplomacy—The act of conducting relations between two or more countries.

Diplomatic recognition—The official acknowledgment of a country's existence by another country.

Electoral college—An assembly elected by the voters to perform the formal duty of electing the president and vice president of the United States.

Embezzlement—The act of stealing money or goods put in one's care for personal use.

Emissaries—An official sent on a specific mission, and responsible for performing a specific duty.

Enlistment—The process of enrolling into the military.

Flank—The right or left side of a military unit or fortified position.

Fortification—Defenses, usually walls and trenches, constructed to add strength to an army's position.

Garrison—Troops inside a fortress.

Hessians—A native of the German region of Hesse who fought as a mercenary for the British army in the Revolutionary War.

Inauguration—An official ceremony inducting an individual into office.

Infantry—Soldiers trained and equipped to fight on foot.

Militia—An army of enlisted citizens that has no officially trained soldiers, as in the regular army; usually called on during an emergency.

Musket—A smooth-bore, long-barreled weapon fired from the shoulder.

Offensive—An attack.

Radical—An individual who desires revolutionary, often violent, changes in a present situation or circumstance.

Recruitment—The process of enlisting people into the military or naval service.

Siege—The surrounding and blockading of a town or a fortress by an army.

Slaughter—To kill in a violent manner, and often to kill a large number of people.

Tactic—In the military, a method of maneuvering forces in combat.

Truce—The suspension of fighting.

Bibliography

Abbott, W. W. Prologue to "An Uncommon Awareness of Self: The Papers of George Washington." (National Archives publication), Spring 1989, pp. 1–15.

Adams, Charles Francis, ed. *Familiar Letters of John Adams and His Wife.* Boston, M.A.: Houghton, Mifflin and Company, 1875.

Adams, James Truslow. *Provincial Society.* Boston, M.A.: Little, Brown, 1933

———. *Revolutionary New England.* Boston: Atlantic Monthly Press, 1923.

Adams, John. *The Works of John Adams.* Vols. 1–10. Charles Francis Adams, ed. Boston, M.A.: Little, Brown & Co., 1850–1856.

Bailyn, Bernard, ed. *Pamphlets of the American Revolution.* Vol. 1, 1750–1765. Cambridge, M.A.: Belknap Press of Harvard University Press, 1965.

Bobrick, Benson. *Angel in the Whirlwind.* New York: Penguin Books, 1997.

Boorstin, Daniel J. *The Americans: The Colonial Experience.* New York: Random House, 1958.

Brookhiser, Richard. *Founding Father.* New York: Free Press, 1998.

Davidson, Marshall B. *The Horizon History of the World in 1776.* New York: Simon & Schuster, 1975.

Fleming, Thomas. *Liberty!* New York: Viking Press, 1997.

Hakim, Joy. *From Colonies to Country 1735–1791.* New York: Oxford University Press, 2003.

Ketchum, Richard M., ed. *The American Heritage Book of the Revolution.* New York: The Macmillian Company, 1974.

Middlekauff, Robert. *The Glorious Cause.* New York: Oxford University Press, 1982.

Munves, James. *Thomas Jefferson and the Declaration of Independence.* Washington, D.C.: Encore Editions, 1976.

Go to the Internet, type the keywords "American Revolution," and you'll get almost two million Web sites dedicated to this subject. From museums to memorabilia, from reenactment events to battlefield sites, the opportunities to learn about and experience the American Revolution are incredible. Below is an admittedly short list of Web site addresses of some of the more useful sites dedicated to the American Revolution. They are listed in alphabetical order.

Battlefields of the Revolution
www.nps.gov/thst/battle.htm
The National Park Service's page that lists all of the American Revolution battlefields, memorials, and historic sites that are part of the National Park Service.

Daughters of the American Revolution
www.dar.org
The Web site for the Daughters of the American Revolution, a nonprofit and educational organization dedicated to the preservation of the memory of those who fought in the American Revolution, and the education of the principles of freedom that formed the foundation of the United States.

George Washington Papers at Library of Congress 1741–1799
www.memory.loc.gov/ammem/gwhtml/gwhome.html
The homepage of the complete George Washington Papers collection from the manuscript division at the Library of Congress, consisting of approximately 65,000 documents.

The History Place: American Revolution
www.historyplace.com/unitedstates/revolution/index.html
A site that lists a number of useful Colonial America, American Revolution, and biography links.

Liberty! The American Revolution
www.pbs.org/ktca/liberty
The online companion site to the six-part PBS documentary on the American Revolution.

The Massachusetts Historical Society
www.masshist.org
The Web site address of the Massachusetts Historical Society. It contains much useful information about Colonial America and the American Revolution.

Monticello: The Home of Thomas Jefferson
www.monticello.org
The Web page of the Thomas Jefferson Foundation dedicated to the preservation and expansion of Monticello, the only home in America on the elite World Heritage List of the United Nations. Contains much useful information on colonial life.

Sons of the American Revolution
www.sar.org
The homepage of the Sons of the American Revolution, a historical, educational, and patriotic organization dedicated to the patriotic principles of the Founding Fathers.

Thomas Jefferson Papers at the Library of Congress
memory.loc.gov/ammem/mtjhtml/mtjhome.html
The complete collection of approximately 27,000 documents of the Thomas Jefferson Papers from the manuscript division of the Library of Congress.

USHistory.org
www.ushistory.org
A "Congress of Web sites" about Colonial America and the American Revolution created and hosted by the Independence Hall Association.

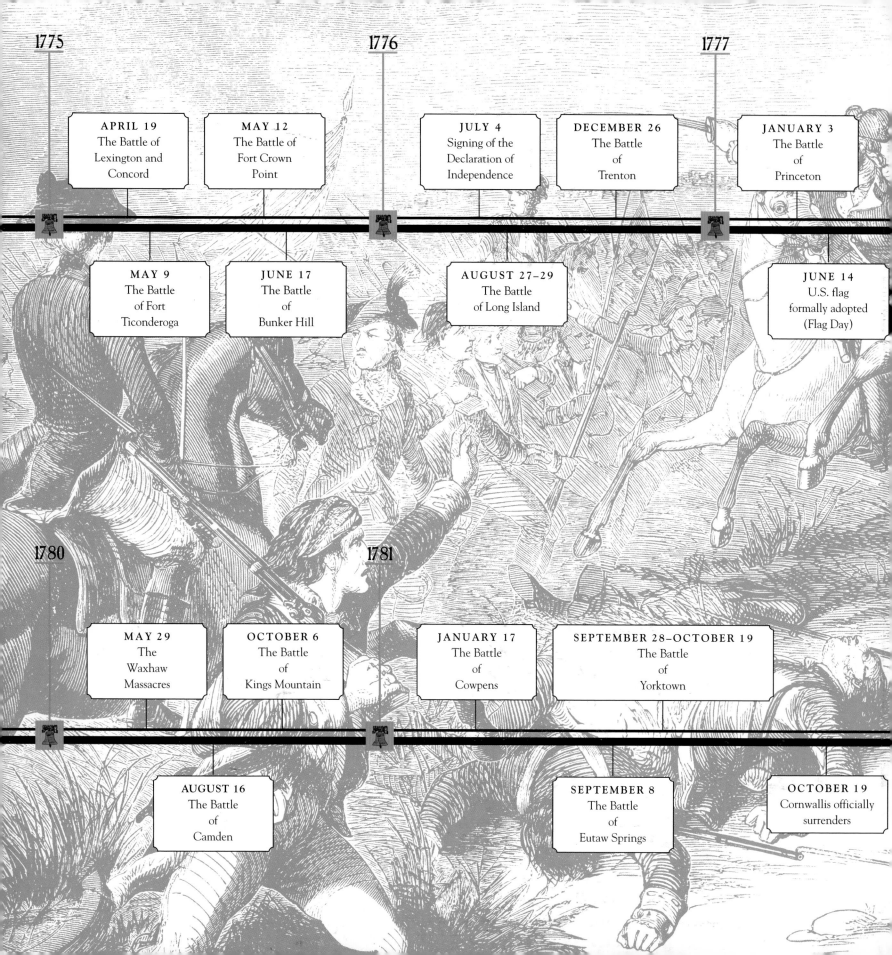

1775

1776

1777

APRIL 19
The Battle of
Lexington and
Concord

MAY 12
The Battle of
Fort Crown
Point

JULY 4
Signing of the
Declaration of
Independence

DECEMBER 26
The Battle
of
Trenton

JANUARY 3
The Battle
of
Princeton

MAY 9
The Battle
of Fort
Ticonderoga

JUNE 17
The Battle
of
Bunker Hill

AUGUST 27–29
The Battle
of Long Island

JUNE 14
U.S. flag
formally adopted
(Flag Day)

1780

1781

MAY 29
The
Waxhaw
Massacres

OCTOBER 6
The Battle
of
Kings Mountain

JANUARY 17
The Battle
of
Cowpens

SEPTEMBER 28–OCTOBER 19
The Battle
of
Yorktown

AUGUST 16
The Battle
of
Camden

SEPTEMBER 8
The Battle
of
Eutaw Springs

OCTOBER 19
Cornwallis officially
surrenders